# Celtic Initials & Alphabets

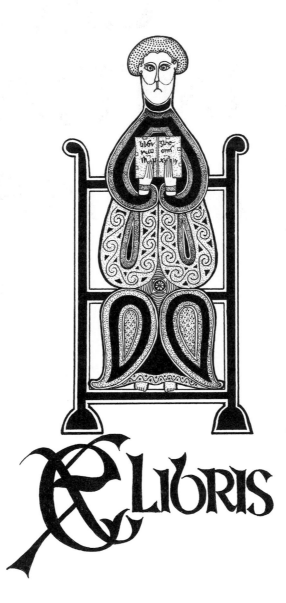

𝕰x Libris

*St Matthew from **The Echternach Gospels***
AD 690, BIBLIOTHÈQUE NATIONALE, PARIS

*Opposite page: Initial from **The Cutbercht Gospels***
EIGHTH CENTURY, NATIONALBIBLIOTHEK, VIENNA

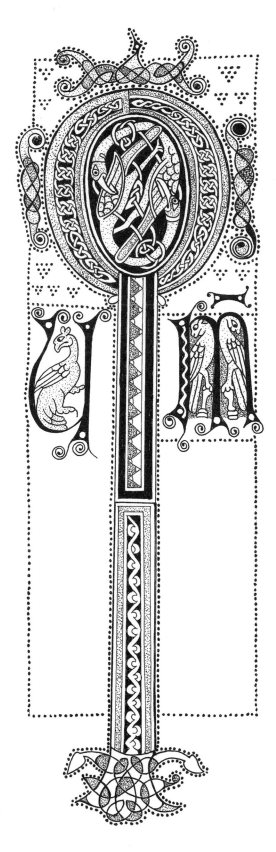

# CELTIC INITIALS & ALPHABETS

## COURTNEY DAVIS

*Additional text by* John Towsey

BLANDFORD

A BLANDFORD BOOK

First published in the UK in 1997
by Blandford, a Cassell imprint
Cassell & Co
Wellington House
125 Strand
London WC2R 0BB

Paperback edition first published in the UK 1999
Reprinted 2000

Distributed in the United States by Sterling Publishing Co.,
Inc., 387 Park Avenue South, New York, NY 10016-8810

A Cataloguing-in-Publication Data entry for this title is
available from the British Library

ISBN 0-7137-2804-3

Designed by Eitetsu Nozawa

Printed and bound in Great Britain by
Hillman Printers (Frome) Ltd, Somerset

# CONTENTS

*Opposite page: Initial from MS Otho CV*
SEVENTH CENTURY, BRITISH MUSEUM, LONDON

*Right: Initial from Durham Gospels A.II.16*
SEVENTH CENTURY, DURHAM CATHEDRAL LIBRARY

# Acknowledgements

I have completed this book in my fiftieth year and so this is naturally a time for me to reflect on the past and on my future.

Since my first scribblings of Celtic art in 1979 and up to the present day, I have been blessed with a group of loyal friends who have helped me through occasionally difficult times and I would like to take this opportunity to thank the following:

Michael and Janet Law

Mike and Laura Elliott

David James

Sue and Pete Riddle

Rudi and Gretchen Diesvelt

Father Dennis O'Neill

Sarah Ross Turner

Johan Quanjer

Beatrice and Laurence Stroud

John, Chris and Charlie Fielder

Grace Elizabeth Brooks

Chris and Fiona Graham Flynn

Val and Bernard Case

Dave Merron

Elaine Gill and David Everett

My thanks as always to my mother, to my beloved Dimity and to my son, Blaine, and also to John Towsey for his excellent work on the research and additional text for this book.

*Top: Initial from Cotton MS, Vespasian A.1*
EIGHTH CENTURY, BRITISH LIBRARY, LONDON

*Opposite page: Initial from St Luke from **The Macdurnan Gospels***
NINTH CENTURY, LAMBETH PALACE, LONDON

*Dedicated to my daughter,*
*Bridie Louise*

# INTRODUCTION

## The Spoken Word and the Written Language

*Initial from* **The Southampton Psalter**
ELEVENTH CENTURY, ST JOHN'S COLLEGE, CAMBRIDGE

The Celts were one of a number of Indo-European tribes who migrated westwards from eastern Europe, eventually inhabiting an area that spread from Galatia in present-day Turkey to Ireland and the Iberian peninsula. They were called Galatai or Keltoi by the Greeks and Galli by the Romans, these names all meaning 'barbarian'. It is from the Greek word Keltoi that our Celt is derived. Since no soft *c* exists in Greek, Celt and Celtic should be pronounced with a hard *k* sound.

The Celts who settled in Galatia to the east spoke the same language as those who migrated westwards to the Atlantic seaboard. This Old Celtic, which originated from the core Ur-language and from the Indo-European language tradition, was close to Italic, the precursor of Latin.

The original wave of Celtic immigrants to the British Isles, known as the q-Celts, spoke Goidelic. They arrived between 2000 and 1200 BC (during the Bronze Age) and displaced or assimilated with the indigenous population, the Ivernians, who had arrived between 4000 and 1600 BC (during the Neolithic period) from the European mainland. When Irish expansion into Pictish Britain occurred and several colonies were established in present-day Wales, the local inhabitants called the newcomers *g wyddel* (savages), from which is derived the term 'Goidelic' for this philological group. The differences between this early Celtic tongue and Italic include the lack of a *p* in Celtic and an *a* in place of the Italic *o*. Goidelic gave rise to three Gaelic languages: Irish, Manx and later Scottish.

A later second wave of Celtic immigration to the British Isles took place during the early Iron Age. Referred to as p-Celts and speaking Brythonic, which gave rise to

Welsh, Cornish and the Breton language of Brittany, these migrants overran most of present-day England. They became the tribes known to the Romans in the last century BC, such as the Brigantes in Yorkshire, the Atrebates in the Thames valley and the Durotriges in Dorset.

The label q-Celts derives from certain differences between this early Celtic tongue and the later p-Celtic. For example, the word *ekvos* in Indo-European, meaning a horse, which in q-Celtic was rendered as *equos*, in p-Celtic became *epos*, the *q* sound being replaced with a *p*. The same holds for the Latin *qui*, meaning who, which in q-Celtic is rendered as *cia* and in p-Celtic as *pwy*. Also the Brython Welsh use the word *ap* for son of, whereas the Goidelic Gaels use the word *mac*.

The Ivernians and the Celts did not have a written language and used different media, such as stone, bone, clay pottery, bronze and iron, to express their culture. Both groups lived side by side after the migrations, as is shown by the continuation of their different funerary practices. The Celts incinerated their dead, whereas the Ivernians favoured burial. An exchange of ideas also occurred, though, as evidenced by the Celts' adoption of chevron patterning on their pottery.

All existing alphabets are probably derived from one original. The word 'alphabet', which appears in Latin as *alphabetum*, was mentioned by St Jerome (c. 340–420) and is formed from the first two letters of the Greek alphabet, alpha and beta. Alpha was derived by the Greeks from the Phoenician vowel sound *a*, which was based on the word *aleph*, meaning an ox, and the written symbol was based on the representation of an ox's head. Beta was derived from the second letter of the Hebrew alphabet, *beth*. Most of the letters of the Greek alphabet are Semitic in origin, and these in turn may have been based on the twenty-four-letter Egyptian alphabet.

The most influential people among the Semitic tribes were the Phoenicians, who lived on the Levantine coast of the Mediterranean in present-day Lebanon and Syria. By 1000 BC they had a thirty-symbol alphabet, each symbol representing a single consonant and entirely abstract. This alphabet was passed on to the Greeks, in the form of twenty-four consonants, before 850 BC.

# Pre-Celtic Alphabets

The earliest Greek script was written from right to left. This was superseded by the Boustrophedon style (following the ox furrow), which consisted of alternate lines from right to left and left to right. However, contemporaneous with both are examples of scripts written from left to right and this style became the norm from around 500 BC. Herodotus (484–425 BC) wrote: 'The Phoenicians . . . introduced into Greece, after their settlement in the country, a number of accomplishments of which the most important was writing, an art unknown to the Greeks.' By 400 BC a standard Greek script, Ionic, had been developed.

The Etruscan alphabet, a direct descendant of the Greek, was used in the area of Italy that corresponds to present-day Tuscany from the seventh to the third centuries BC. When the Romans defeated the Etruscans and took power in Italy in the second century BC, they adopted the twenty-one letters of the Etruscan alphabet and added two more.

# Celtic Monasticism and Book Production

In the year AD 400 most northern Europeans worshipped one or more non-Christian gods. Attacks on such pagan worship by clerics like St Martin, the Bishop of Tours, had only just begun and monasticism was almost unknown. Within 500 years most of Europe was Christian and monasticism was the most important spiritual and cultural force.

The early Celtic saint was essentially a celibate and a hermit, choosing the wildest and most inaccessible places from which to devote himself to a life of seclusion and self-denial. Such spots became the start of monastic schools which then, in turn, developed into great centres of learning. St Ninian, for example, after visiting St Martin of Tours, came to Scotland, landing at Whithorn, between 410 and 432, and built a stone church in a style unusual among the Britons, dedicating it to St Martin.

The relatively few 'barbarian' Christians were the subject of missions sent out from Rome by the Popes – for example, Pope Celestine sent Palladius to Ireland in 431 – to help strengthen their faith. Palladius found that the existing monasticism was based on the example of Thebaid, who had sought spiritual perfection through solitude, penance and fasting, and on the model of the monastery at Lérins, near Cannes. To these monastery cells came people seeking temporal and spiritual guidance. One such

*Chi-Rho Monogram, **Ussher Codex 1***
SEVENTH CENTURY, TRINITY COLLEGE, DUBLIN

Christian was Patrick, who was the first to see that his moral duty lay outside the empire in converting the pagans. He attempted to start in Ireland, partly by establishing monasteries, which became important institutions, acting as centres for missionary activity, for basic education in the common written language (Latin), for book production and for the training of clergy.

As the numbers and sizes of these monasteries increased through grants of land, they became economic and political centres as well. The power of the bishops' sees was overshadowed by the monastic abbots' influence. Land grants were becoming so contentious that both clerical and secular organizations recognized the need to reach a compromise to diffuse mounting tension. This was achieved through the kinship system, whereby relatives of lay donors had a stake in the monastery. By the end of the sixth century the Irish Church had become a church of monks.

The Irish monasteries of the sixth and seventh centuries were not very imposing buildings, comprising a circular enclosure within which stood a few rectangular wooden structures with thatched or shingled roofs and a cluster of round wattle huts with, perhaps, a tall, roughly hewn slab of stone near the door of the church.

One of the objectors to the kinship system from the clerical ranks was Columbanus, who, in 590, decided to go on a major pilgrimage. With twelve companions, he left Ireland for the Continent. He founded a number of monasteries in Gaul – for example, at Luxeuil – and eventually reached northern Italy, where he founded a monastery at Bobbio. His model of large, rural monasteries free from episcopal interference appealed to the rulers of Gaul and within fifty years of his death large numbers of monasteries had been established.

In c. 565 Columba, who was from a similar background to Columbanus, went with his followers north from Ireland to the south-west of Scotland, where he founded the monastery at Iona. This was to be the base for the monks of Scotia, who were eclectic rather than missionary, although their monasteries were also the foundations for future missions. Iona became a major centre for insular monasticism and, as a

*Script from* **The Cathach**
AD 591–7, ROYAL IRISH ACADEMY, DUBLIN

seat of learning, played host to a number of notables in the early seventh century. One of these was Oswald, who, on becoming king of Northumbria in 635, sent to Iona for clerics to convert his subjects. Aidan arrived in answer to the king's call and he established the monastery at Lindisfarne. It seems to have been the general practice in England that a king or a lay dignitary funded the establishment of a monastery, whether as a thanksgiving for events in this life or in preparation for the hereafter. Such patronage was of major importance in the spread of monastic centres.

Meanwhile, Pope Gregory's mission, starting with St Augustine in Canterbury *c.* 597, moved northwards and eventually founded an episcopal see at York – in 627. However, it was not until after the Synod of Whitby in 664 that the new connections with Rome and the existing Irish links through Iona and Lindisfarne bore artistic fruit. The resulting explosion of home-produced illuminated manuscripts, augmented by additions from Rome and other continental centres, heralded a new Golden Age.

European intellectual life throughout the early Middle Ages was focused mostly in the monasteries. Copies of important texts, both Christian and classical, were made in their scriptoria and many had their own libraries. In respect of the magnificence of illumination and calligraphic expertise, book production had reached its peak by the end of the ninth century with *The Book of Kells*. Other notable codices are *The Book of Durrow*, *The Lindisfarne Gospels*, *The Lichfield Gospels* and *The Echternach Gospels*, and there were plenty of fine works being produced throughout Britain and Europe. This scale of production might have continued indefinitely had it not been for the disruption caused by the Viking raids throughout the eighth and ninth centuries in both Ireland and England. For example, the monastery at Iona, which had produced so many books, had to be abandoned in 806, and the Northumbrian monastic centres at Lindisfarne, which had produced *The Lindisfarne Gospels*, and neighbouring Monkwearmouth and Jarrow, which had produced many books under the auspices of the Venerable Bede, had been abandoned by 876.

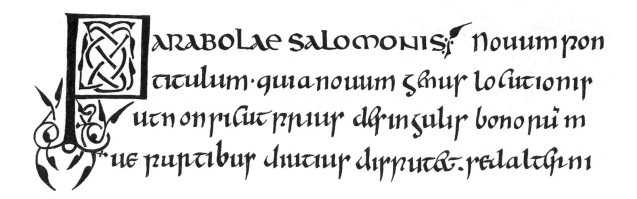

*The Venerable Bede's commentary on the Book of Proverbs*
EIGHTH CENTURY, BODLEIAN LIBRARY, OXFORD

Now that, under the auspices of Theodore of Canterbury, the Church had become firmly established in England, the energies of more idealistic clergy began to turn outwards towards the Continent and their German cousins. Wihtberht went to Frisia, as did Willibrord (he became the first bishop of Utrecht), while Hewals went to Saxony and martyrdom, and Swithberht to Bructeri. However, the most successful at this time was Boniface, who in central Germany established the Bavarian see, presided over Frankish councils, unified the Church and firmly established the Pope of Rome's control. By 785 missionaries under the protection of Charlemagne had converted the Saxons.

Clearly this missionary zeal, from Ireland in the first instance and then from England and Rome, carried with it the inspiration for the writing of Gospels, the focus of the services in the churches, along with the establishment of scriptoria for the production of these books.

The Frankish manuscripts draw entirely on late Roman motifs and contemporary eastern ornament. Slightly earlier than those of Northumbria are the manuscripts now in the Dombibliothek (Cathedral Library) at Cologne. It was not until the first half of the eighth century that the characteristic style appears – good examples are the Gothic missal in the Vatican Library, Rome (c. 700), *The Chronicle of Fredegar* in the Bibliothèque Nationale, Paris (c. 715), and *The Gundohinus Gospels* in Autun, written at Fleury (754). This style was characterized by bright colours, lively drawings (almost part of the written word, not separate), depictions of animals, birds and fish, often forming the initial capital itself, and extensive use of compass and ruler. It may well have been derived from northern Italy (possibly Bobbio), via monks returning from the east, but it also contained neo-insular designs such as intricate interlace, and animals with interlaced legs and tails. There was movement between monasteries: Alcuin, for example, a British scholar, studied at a Celtic monastery in Tours at this time.

# ALPHABETS

ihscogitationeseo

rum,respondens

dixitadillos

*Text from MS Add. 5463*
EIGHTH–NINTH CENTURY,
BRITISH MUSEUM, LONDON

## Uncial Script

The spread of Christianity throughout the provinces of the Roman Empire following the emperor Constantine's conversion in 313 was the prime medium for the adoption of the Roman alphabet in western Europe. Christian missionaries such as St Patrick and St Augustine brought with them knowledge of a written language, so that by the end of the sixth century there were at least two book-hands in the British Isles. One of these was the Irish majuscule or half-uncial and the other was the Roman uncial script. The latter was a true pen form of writing which, together with the innovation of vellum, enabled scribes to write more clearly and much more quickly. These developments, together with factors such as patronage, meant that book production increased. Benedict took several of his imported books to the twin monasteries of Monkwearmouth and Jarrow in north-east England, so that by the end of the seventh century libraries had been established.

The alphabet above shows the most common form of the uncial script adopted. The derivation of the term 'uncial' is thought to relate to the fact that the letters were an inch in height. The Old English *ynce* meaning a twelfth part probably comes from the Latin *uncia*, which is the twelfth part of one *pes* (a foot), and/or from *ynce* when it refers to the width of a thumb. The text is known as *scriptura continua* – that is, with no letter separation or word division, and no punctuation, which added to the speed of writing. The different lengths of line indicated where the orator could pause and perhaps change emphasis, a system which is known as *per cola et commata*. Very few abbreviations were used, especially within the body of the text. Distinctive forms include the *A* with a thorn-like bow, a rounded *d* with the ascender bent back over the counter, the rounded *m* and our capital *B*. The upper-case letters are the basis for the versal capitals and major initial pages of the Gospels.

# abcderʒhıl mnopqrstu vxȥ

*Script from **The Lindisfarne Gospels***
AD 700, BRITISH LIBRARY, LONDON

# Lindisfarne Half-uncial Script

From the sixth century onwards there developed from the Roman uncial a smaller and more cursive form of script which is called half-uncial. The letters were roughly half the size of the uncials and had more ascenders and descenders rising and falling below the writing line. The smaller script allowed more variations of letter form, such as the Irish majuscule and the English majuscule. The term majuscule is taken from the Latin word *majusculus*, which is a diminutive of the word *major*, meaning bigger – that is, bigger than 'minuscule', which is its lower-case counterpart. The letters mark the transition from the use of the more cumbersome uncial to the speedier forms of minuscule.

The English majuscule or half-uncial developed in the monastery at Lindisfarne and had a powerful advocate in the form of Bishop Eadfrith, who used it in the majestic *Lindisfarne Gospels* codex, written around the year 700. Eadfrith, who wrote the codex, rigidly adhered to the headlines and baselines, to the breadth, the roundness and the slight thickening of the letter form, made with the use of a broader nibbed quill. The nibs were cut to a consistent width throughout the execution of the text and were held parallel to the guidelines drawn across the page. Even so, this well-mannered and orderly script still employed some uncial characters, possibly due to the influence of the nearby Monkwearmouth and Jarrow monasteries, which were still using uncial script. The uncial forms used include *R*, *S* and *N*, which are upper-case letters, alongside their lower-case counterparts. Some of the lower-case letters are minuscule forms, among which are the straight *d*, the *e* and the curved *l*.

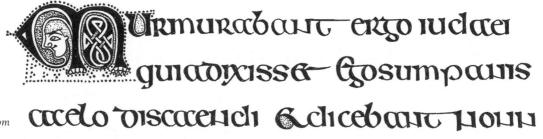

# Kells Half-uncial Script

The Irish majuscule had no native Irish book-hand from which to evolve and owes its existence to the Latin half-uncial form, which may have had its roots in Franco-Lombardic styles. The script is slightly slimmer and narrower than its English counterpart which makes the wedge serifs, a major characteristic, more prominent. It reached its peak in *The Book of Kells*, which was probably written around 800.

It is a rounded hand with the bowl of the letters *o* and *b* being circular but still slightly slimmer at the poles. The bar of the enclosed *e* counter is extended horizontally, but still as a serif terminal, as with the backwards-bending ascender of the *d*. The letter *s* is often represented by a form similar to the modern lower-case *r*, whereas the *r* proper is in the form of a modern upper-case *R*. The *y* appears to dance across the page, as does the *g*, but the *n* and the *u* are squat and immovable. The *a* is type formed by the ligature of the *o* and *c*, and the *z* is very eccentric.

abcdefghi

lmnopqrst

uvxyz

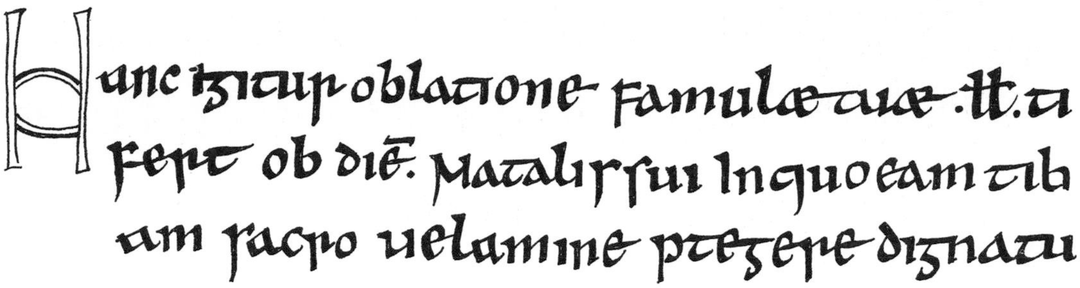

# Minuscule

The *Collins English Dictionary* defines 'minuscule' as 'a lower-case letter… a small cursive 7th-century style of lettering derived from the uncial… from Latin minuscula "very small"'. There are a number of different forms of this minuscule book-hand: for example, the Carolingian, the insular set, the insular hybrid and the insular cursive. This latter form of running hand was first developed in Ireland and was originally used for business and legal documents and for transcribing less formal books. It was also commonly used for glosses to the main text: for example, Aldred used it for the writing of his gloss on a copy of Bede's commentary on the Book of Proverbs, written in the second half of the eighth century.

The thinness of the letter form suggests a fine quill, perhaps a crow's feather, as if the scribe was concerned about using too much ink or the document did not warrant a lot of time and vellum, as with the Gospel codices. Clearly the hand was built for speed and not refinement. The ascenders still retained the serif terminals, as do the shoulders at the top of the stems of the *m*, *n*, *f*, *s* and *i*. The descenders, however, tend to end in a point. The *b* and *d* are now opposites, as are the *p* and *q*, similar to those in modern lower-case script.

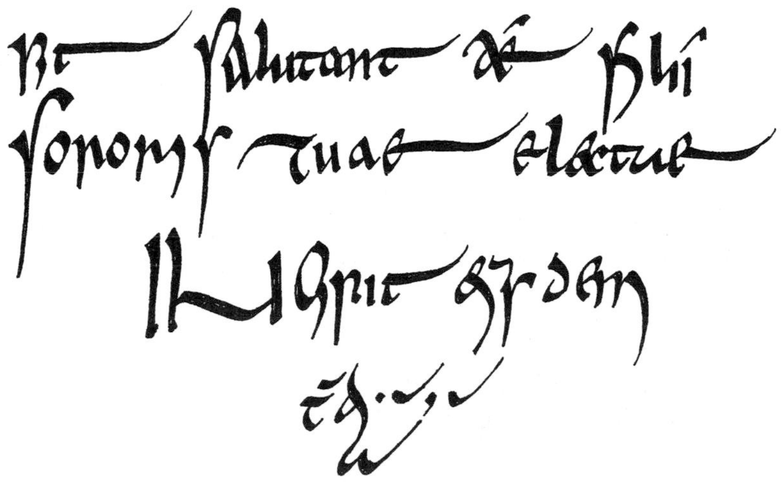

*Script above from*
***Durham Rituale***
TENTH CENTURY,
DURHAM CATHEDRAL LIBRARY

*and left from*
***The Book of Armagh***
AD 807,
TRINITY COLLEGE, DUBLIN

# FAITHDIEGUNHERD

## Kells Half-uncial and Angular Capitals

In addition to the major initial letters of the illuminated pages and the script of the text, the codices contained smaller capital letters, most of which occurred as continuation lettering. These smaller capitals, or display script, show a variety and diversity of form not only from one group of related codices to another but also within each group and within each codex. Two forms are recognizable, one rounded in outline and the other angular. The capitals above are the angular form, with the stems, arms and crossbars more often than not straight lines meeting at right angles. There is a slight variation at the serif terminals and the occasional curved bowl of an *S* and a *C*, but the overall structure is angular. The three parallel stems and the crossbars of the *M* strongly emphasize this form, as do the many variations of the letter *A*. Even the letter *O* is drawn as a diamond shape using straight sides.

In the lettering below the crossbar(s) of the letter *A* have been taken a stage further in that they have been extended into a knotwork pattern, but they have still retained the angular characteristic. Other letters, such as the *O* which has a counter filled with angular knotwork and the crossbar of the *M* which is similarly drawn, have at times been drawn to this pattern.

*Angular script from* The Book of Kells
AD 800, TRINITY COLLEGE, DUBLIN

*Detail from the beginning of St Matthew's Gospel, **The Book of Kells***
AD 800, TRINITY COLLEGE, DUBLIN

*Detail from the beginning of St Luke's Gospel,* **The Lindisfarne Gospels**
AD 700, British Library, London

# Lindisfarne Display Script

T he continuation lettering, or display script, opposite comes from a major insular codex of the eighth century. The style of the script is predominantly angular but it does incorporate features, such as the bowls of the letters *P* and *R*, of the rounded form. The rounding of the *U* enables it to be distinguished easily from the *V*, which is angular in form. In addition to these regular features there is the decoration of the capitals, infrequently used in the less important codices. Here, different forms of spiral terminals are used to great effect, as is the incorporation of bird's heads, often with spiral crests. One example of the letter *O* which is angular in form has cut-offs where the apex of each of the four buttress triangles is extended into biting bird's heads. The counter of the same *O* is filled with perfectly drawn interlace. All the letters are outlined in black lines and/or in red dots.

*Detail from the beginning of St John's Gospel,* **The Lindisfarne Gospels**
AD 700, BRITISH LIBRARY, LONDON

*Initials from MS Cod. F.v.1.8*
EIGHTH CENTURY,
ST PETERSBURG PUBLIC LIBRARY

# St Petersburg

**m**any of the insular manuscripts have the introductory pages to each of the four Gospels in the form of major initials: the 'Liber…' in St Matthew, the 'Initium…' in St Mark, the 'Quoniam…' in St Luke and the 'In principio…' in St John. These major initials were followed by continuation lettering which was commonly in the form of decorated, but smaller, capital letters – that is, display script. These capital letters were treated to embellishment by the scribe/illuminator to the extent that they formed a style of their own. The continuation letters were sufficiently numerous in any one codex to form an alphabet and style often unique to that codex. Thus there is a great range of aesthetically different types of lettering. For example, the *'Liber…'* initial page found in St Matthew's Gospel had the continuation capitals *'generationis Ihu Xpi fili David'* in all the same style, which was also the style of the capitals on the other initial pages. The capitals shown above were outlined in strong and brilliant black, with the interior of the letter line patterned variously but leaving a white line in reserve next to the outline, throwing it into relief. These letters, therefore, did not need a coloured panel. The tapering stems, the concave serif terminals, the use of spirals as finial extensions and the swelling of the bowls of the letters give a pattern of moving, interlocking outlines to this otherwise flat and abstract pattern. The emptiness of the background on which the letters are drawn is partially filled with red-dot outlining and triangular groups of red dots.

*Initials from **The Douce Psalter, 176***
EIGHTH–NINTH CENTURY, BODLEIAN LIBRARY, OXFORD

# Merovingian

**W**hile the insular scribes, artists and illuminators were pursuing a geometric approach to their manuscripts, their continental counterparts were developing a different style. In present-day northern France, in what may be called Gaul, a Frankish dynasty, founded by Clovis I, ruled from about 500 to 750. These were the Merovingians, and their scribes and illuminators turned their letters, based on the Italian style represented by the extant fifth-century codex Vatican Virgil, into birds, fish and other zoomorphs. These were to be the ancestors of the great proliferation of zoomorphic and anthropomorphic forms of the next 1,000 years. This style is more drawing than lettering, since the letters are formed from images of men and animals.

The capital letters of the eighth-century Merovingian artist/scribes are often circular in form, with, for example, a *C* being an incomplete circle given a second dimension by the addition of arcs of other circles across its upper and lower curves and its back. These then became fishes in the imagination of the artist. The letter *U* has two fish-arcs for stems which metamorphose into two Ionic capitals posing as serifs. The bird-like bowl of the letter *D* would have been circular, had not the artist/scribe decided that the fish could become the stem of the letter, and the tail of the *Q* literally became the merged tails of the two fish enclosing the counter of the letter. All of these initials are vividly coloured.

A second characteristic of these letters which also goes back to the Vatican Virgil is that they are drawn in outline. The shapes are built up using the enclosing lines, whether they are outlines of different abstract patterns or are zoomorphic in origin. Sometimes the letters are plain outline; sometimes they are in one or more colours; and sometimes they are checked, striped or patterned. As we have seen, they often turn into birds or fish. These creatures are totally unrealistic because the artist has made the shape, which may be bird- or fish-like, and filled it in with anatomical features of birds and fish. The fish was the earliest Christian symbol for Christ and the soul. This is thought to have come about because the letters of the Greek word for fish, *ichthus*, are the first letters in each word of the phrase 'Jesus Christ, the son of God, Saviour'.

*Top left:*
*Initial from*
**Vallicelliana B62**
EIGHTH CENTURY,
VATICAN, ROME

*Top right:*
*Initial from*
**MS 9850**
EIGHTH CENTURY,
BIBLIOTHÈQUE
ROYALE, BRUSSELS

*Bottom left:*
*Initial from*
**Add.31031**
EIGHTH CENTURY,
BRITISH LIBRARY,
LONDON

*Bottom right:*
*Initial from*
**Corpus Christi 193**
EIGHTH CENTURY,
CORPUS CHRISTI
COLLEGE,
CAMBRIDGE

# A B C D E O P Q R S T V

*Letters from **The Benedictional of St Ethelwold*** AD 980, BIBLIOTHÈQUE MUNICIPALE, ROUEN

## The Benedictional of St Ethelwold

**α** lthough not strictly speaking a Celtic form of alphabet, the initial letters in the late-tenth-century *Benedictional of St Ethelwold* show the lasting influence of the Roman origins on the style of the insular alphabets, even though the uncial script was no longer in favour. The capitals of this collection of episcopal blessings are between one and three inches high, drawn in gold and may have been painted in freehand.

The basic forms are square capitals, but the fact that the letters are drawn and not cut out with a chisel gives a much stronger contrast between thin and thick lines, and a freer movement in the definition of the curves. The stems are not straight parallels but move in wide curves throughout their length. The serifs are fine strokes drawn across the arcs of the curves, neatly cutting them off. Curves move out from the stems in great sweeps, rising slightly above them in order to make wider bowls. With letters like the *O* and the *Q*, the bowls are created by hair strokes which swell in girth and move back into slimness. The letters *N* and *L*, among others, show the elegance of the fine line in their tapering limbs. In the letters *A* and *M*, the pointed apex of the classical lines has been replaced with a horizontal serif which cuts across the wide stroke before it reaches a point. The lettering has a classical perfection.

*Initial from Cotton MS,*
*Vespasian A.1*
EIGHTH CENTURY, BRITISH LIBRARY,
LONDON

# Illuminated Manuscripts

The word 'manuscript' is derived from the Latin words *manus* (hand) and *scriptus*, from *scribere* (to write), and is used to refer to any handwritten text. Illumination, from the Latin *illuminare* (to adorn) refers to the hand-painted decoration in a manuscript, usually employing brilliant colours. Illuminations took the form of decorated letters, borders and figurative scenes, also called miniatures (from the Latin, *miniare*, meaning to colour with red, because the adornment of the books was originally executed in red lead or *minium*).

The most elaborate and beautiful illumination was devoted to religious works, which, until the rise of the universities in the twelfth century, were produced in monasteries. The main insular monastic scriptoria were Iona/Kells, Lindisfarne,

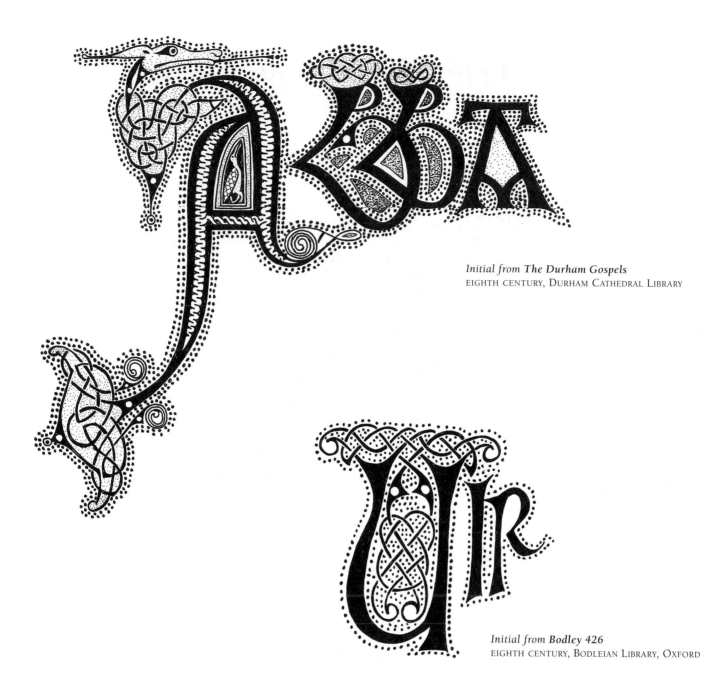

*Initial from **The Durham Gospels***
EIGHTH CENTURY, DURHAM CATHEDRAL LIBRARY

*Initial from **Bodley 426***
EIGHTH CENTURY, BODLEIAN LIBRARY, OXFORD

Monkwearmouth/Jarrow, Canterbury, Winchester and York. To produce their manuscripts, the following procedures were adopted by the monks and scribes:

1. the sheets of vellum were prepared;

2. the text was written in, leaving space for decoration;

3. the coloured writing, capitals and line-finishings were added;

4. the illumination of the initials, line-finishings and borders was undertaken;

5. the book was bound.

# Insular Gospels

The great Gospel books, or codices, of the insular scriptoria were the peak of manuscript production and those which were to be used on the altar were lavishly decorated. The illuminated letters opposite form the word '*Liber*', which was often used on the opening page of the Gospel of St Matthew, the first of the four Gospels in the Vulgate version. The whole illumination consisted of the words '*Liber generationis Ihu Xpi fili David*', which translated reads, 'the book of generations of Jesus Christ, the son of David'. The '*Liber*' described here covered approximately 50 per cent of the ten by eight inch area of writing on folio eighteen of the Gospel.

The letters are outlined in strong and brilliant black, with the interior of the letter line patterned variously but leaving a white line in reserve next to the outline, throwing it into relief. The patterned surface enclosed by the outline is enhanced by the use of colours – pale blue, yellow green and reddish brown. The fluid two-dimensional nature of its conception is particularly apparent in the way in which the substance of the *E* seems to flow into that of the *R*. It is a drawing, a flat abstract pattern of moving, interlocking outlines, with dots used to encompass the letters and to scatter in the interstices, especially the 'triangles' of dots which represent the Holy Trinity. The versal letter *L* has irregularly shaped and sized panels of zoomorphic features and interlace. Six of the seven panels are filled with an animal and interlace pattern, while the seventh has two birds and interlace. Snakes may be represented in two of the panels. The head of the letter terminates in double-coil spirals connected by black single-line interlace. The base of the letter has finials which are continued as black interlace into the counter and into the area of the folio below the *ER* of the word '*Liber*'. The letter is enclosed by a single line of red dots.

The letter *I* sits in the open counter of the *L* and contains a full-length panel of knotwork, with the head terminal of two gaping birds' heads whose tongues extend as wire into the letter *B* and the deer-like form respectively. The base of the *I* terminates in the form of an animal head with gaping mouth and fangs, the tongue of which extends into single-line interlace. The bowls of the letter *B* are filled with knotwork and terminate in gaping animal heads, with teeth and extended tongues, as with the base of the stem. The stem is filled with a panel of bird and interlace. The crossbar of the letter *E* is occupied by two back-to-back birds which are intertwined with two other sinuous birds coming from the head and foot bars, which terminate in a scroll. This then flows into the *R*, which has panels of interlace and birds. Each letter flows into the next as a continuous stream of movement. Finally, the illuminator filled the rest of the counter of the *L* with a deer-like animal form.

*Beginning of St Matthew's Gospel, MS Lat.F.V.i.N.8*
EIGHTH CENTURY, ST PETERSBURG PUBLIC LIBRARY

*Detail from **The Gospel of St Gatien***
EIGHTH CENTURY, BIBLIOTHÈQUE NATIONALE,
PARIS

# Brittany

This major initial from the opening page of *The Gospel of St Gatien* is in a sumptuous Gospel book in Celtic style produced in Brittany in the eighth or ninth century. The text of the first page comprises the initials *IN*, followed by the continuation lettering '*principio er/at verbum et ve/rbum erat a [pie]/ud dm. et ds. erat verbum*', which translates as In the beginning was the word and the word was with God and God was the word.' These capitals are in black ink on a coloured panel; the colours used on this page are green, orange and yellow.

The stem of the initial is made up of the *I* and the left-hand upright of the *N*. It has coloured panels, all of equal width but irregular in length and alternating colour. The panels are included to break up the stem, which would ordinarily be thick and cumbersome. The lines of the margins of the panels are in black ink and are bounded by white, double-line interlace. These are broken up by two double sets and one single set of knots in the interlace. The base of the stem terminates in a concave serif in which sits a complex pattern of interlace, on coloured grounds, forming the bodies of two birds and extending as the neck and head of the same birds. The birds are biting their necks – a common feature of insular manuscript bird designs. The two halves of the complex form a mirror image.

Between the stems of the *N* are two panels. One is occupied by a deer-like animal whose tail and one ear extend as elbowed, knotted interlace on a coloured background. The other panel has a rectangular window of white elbowed and knotted interlace on a black background, set in a white frame on a coloured ground. This coloured ground enclosing the window is framed in white with a single black line running

*Initial from* **The Gospel of St Gatien**
EIGHTH CENTURY, BIBLIOTHÈQUE NATIONALE, PARIS

up through it, which breaks up the thick whiteness of the frame. The frame continues into the mass of elbowed and knotted interlace, on a coloured background, which covers the whole of the top of the initial. This interlace has two scrolled terminals, both occupied by forward-looking human faces. The stem of the upright has regular panels terminating at the base in another complex of mirrored-image interlace. The whole of the initial is enclosed by a double row of orange dots.

# The Scriptoria of Southern England

**D**uring the second half of the eighth century, a number of de luxe Gospel books were produced in scriptoria in southern England. These scriptoria used insular and continental manuscripts as models in their ornamentation.

The versal capital opposite is the *Q* at the beginning of St Luke's Gospel in one of these southern English manuscripts. The tail of the stem is drawn down into the uncial text of the Gospel almost like a descender. Gospels in this series commonly had a panel after the initial where the continuation capitals of the rest of the introduction were written. This was instead of the whole-page initial, which was more common in the seventh and eighth centuries Gospel codices. The illuminator, although drawing the lines for the margins of the box of the panel, did not write in the capitals. Thus left out were the words '*conati sunt ordinare*'.

*Initial from **Canonici Patr. Lat. 112***
EIGHTH–NINTH CENTURY, BODLEIAN LIBRARY, OXFORD

The versal letter *Q* has a panel stem. All the panels are surrounded by colour ground, which in turn has a thick black line as its margin. Within the panels from the top to the bottom are an eagle biting elbowed interlace, a dog whose ears and tail extend as interlace, a long-legged bird whose crest extends as interlace, a mythical creature whose tail and tongue extend as interlace and finally, in the half-panel, another bird. The nib-like base of the stem extends into interlace, which is almost layered in appearance, with elbow knots and an animal-head terminal. The head of the stem ends as elbow interlace, which is the extended tail of a running dog.

In the counter of the letter is a toothed biting lion's head with a dolphin in its jaws. The hollow ground of the bow of the letter is filled with panels which taper. Two panels contain birds, two contain elbow-knotted interlace, two are part-bird and part-interlace and the central, largest panel contains an animal. The panels have on both sides a black ground on which has been drawn small coloured diamond shapes. The lower part of the bow extends as the body of the lion and contains large, white dots on a black background. The fillings of the *Q* were set on coloured panels that seem to have been gold leaf which has been scraped off.

This would certainly have made the Gospel a de luxe edition. The whole of the initial is enclosed in a double row of orange dots and the colours used were orange, green and blue.

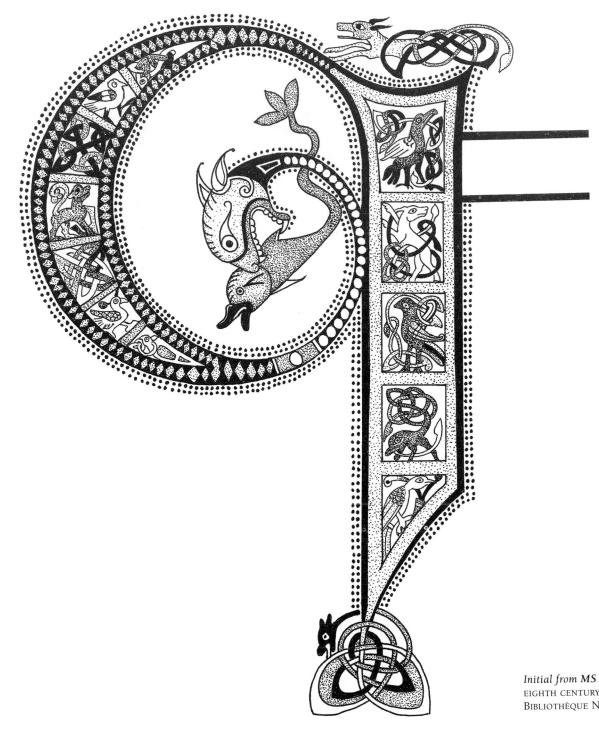

*Initial from MS 281*
EIGHTH CENTURY,
BIBLIOTHÈQUE NATIONALE, PARIS

*St Matthew from **The Book of Dimma***
EIGHTH CENTURY, TRINITY COLLEGE, DUBLIN

# Irish Pocket Gospels

The initial opposite comes from one of a group of Irish pocket Gospels and is the '*IN p*' of the opening of St John's Gospel. The initial is set into the left-hand margin of the text and extends nearly to the bottom of the text area, taking up some twenty-five of the twenty-nine lines on the page. The page measures approximately six and a half by five and a half inches. The script of the text is written in Irish minuscule.

Several of these late-eighth-century pocket books are extant. They are written in minuscule text with numerous abbreviations, which gives a cramped appearance; no doubt the priority was to get as much text as possible on to the relatively small page. This enabled the scribe/illuminator to keep the Gospel book small and light to carry. The books were very practical and this style continued in production right into the twelfth century, some 400 years later.

In relation to the size of the page on which it was drawn, our initial is very elaborate. The thick black stems of the *I* and left-hand upright of the *N* are separated by a hollow filled with large white dots on a black background with a thin white border. The combined stems taper towards the base, where they terminate in a large head of a bird which has a exaggerated crest with a lobed terminal. Each of the heads of the combined stems terminate in large wedge serifs, the blackness of which has been reduced by the inclusion of a small, white triangular eye.

Between the two sets of uprights the bar of the *N* has been drawn into a mosaic, similar to a maze. This key pattern in black, with white and coloured borders, has a pathway outlined in orange-red dots. In fact, the whole of the initial is encompassed within orange-red dots.

The shorter uprights of the right-hand stem of the *N* and the stem of the *P* are similar to their larger neighbours, but the hollow between them is filled with black dots on a white background, the reverse of that of their neighbours. The wedge serifs at the head do not appear to contain any features, unlike those at the base, which have short, toe-like terminals similar to the half-circles drawn at the heads of the larger stems of their neighbours.

The bowl of the *P* extends in one direction out across the top of the initial, terminating in a black triangle, and in the other direction it joins the stem about one-third of the way down its length. The counter is filled with black ink outlined in white, with a bowl of white dots. There is also this curious extra superfluous smaller bowl, which is drawn as an extension of the necessary larger one perhaps to break up the letter line of the stem of the *p*. As the letter *r* is written in the body of the text, it cannot be the tail or leg of that letter.

The whole of the feature conveys a solidity of purpose.

# Armagh

The word Armagh comes from Ard Macha or Macha's Height, Macha being a pagan queen who built a fort on a hill. The city claims to go back to the time of St Patrick and the ecclesiastical lawyers of the town claimed, in the seventh-century *Liber Angeli*, that because St Patrick was the Apostle of the Irish, God rewarded him and his church of Armagh with precedence over all the churches and monasteries of Ireland. The church claimed to have relics of St Peter and St Paul, a relic of the Roman martyr St Lawrence and, by secret dispensation, a linen cloth stained with the blood of Christ.

Armagh had a productive scriptorium during the eighth and ninth centuries. The finest extant manuscript is *The Book of Armagh*, written around 807 by the scribe Ferdomnach under the direction of the Abbot Torbach. The Annals tells us that Ferdomnach died in 844 or 846. *The Book of Armagh* is made up of three parts: documents in Latin and Irish relating to St Patrick, the New Testament and *The Life of St Martin*. The manuscript has good-quality ornamentation, with line drawings of the Evangelists' symbols and elegant wire initials. A cumtach was made for the book at the orders of Donnchad, King of Tara, son of Flann, in or around 937.

The New Testament section of *The Book of Armagh* is made up of readings from the four Gospels, each of which has a major initial as part of its introduction page. The representative initial here is the '*IN p*' of the '*In principio erat verbum et verbum erat apud deum et deus erat verbum*', which translates as, 'In the beginning was the word and the word was with God and God was the word.' This is the introduction to St John's Gospel. The initial extends for thirty-one of the thirty-five lines of the page, each folio is a maximum of seven and a half by five and a half inches, and the script is written in two-columned Irish minuscule.

The '*IN*' forms a monogram, a feature of early-ninth-century Irish manuscripts, but is a simple pen-and-ink drawing, which is unusual for such an important book from that era. The left-hand upright is comprised of the capital *I* and the left stem of the *N*. The drawing has a bold, black line which is hollow and filled with white, thus reducing the heaviness of the letter. The base of the combined stems of the letters widens and the cupola is occupied by elbow-knotted interlace, which is drawn down to terminate in a pelta with its outer corners elaborated into double-coil spirals. Similarly, the head of the stems widens and the cupola is occupied by elbow-knotted interlace with lobed terminals. Two elbows extend upwards and have a ring at their apex. An unusual feature is that the bar of the *N* is a straight, bold black line. The inner right-hand stem forms the shorter upright of the *N* and the outer is its counterpart in the form of the stem of the *p* of the word '*principio*'. The combined head of the two stems is a mirror image of the longer left-hand uprights, but the serifs of the base cupola extend as single black-line interlace, not double. The bowl of the letter *p* is rectangular and like a large window surround, with a smaller framed window within. Perhaps the smaller window was supposed to have a pattern drawn within it, as with other similar capitals. The continuation letters of the '*principio*' are written as very small upper-case minuscule script. The counter between the two sets of uprights of the monogram is filled with two inward-facing peacocks whose crests extend as interlace both to the front and to the rear. This interlace flows through the hollows in the stems out from the boundary of the initial. There are no coloured dots used in the major initials – another unusual feature of this manuscript.

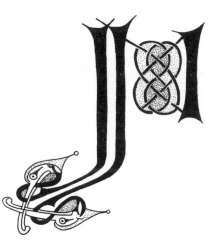

*Initial from **St Luke's Gospel**,*
***The Durham Gospels***
EIGHTH CENTURY, DURHAM CATHEDRAL LIBRARY

# The Northumbrian Centres

**m**any manuscripts were written in the Northumbrian centres of Lindisfarne and Monkwearmouth and Jarrow before they were sacked by Vikings and finally abandoned in the ninth century.

The two initials on the opposite page come from one of these centres and were drawn in a Gospel codex in the early eighth century. The Gospels were vital liturgical accessories for any churchman or religious community at this time. The proliferation of bishoprics and monasteries in the late seventh and early eighth centuries must have necessitated the creation of numerous Gospel books of modest artistic status, many of which have not survived to this day. These initials are examples of the very simple decoration which was common in such Gospels.

The *I* is not very striking when taking into account the great significance of the Gospels to the clergy. It is the initial letter at the beginning of the Gospel of St John and the rest of the introduction is very ordinary. So in the '*In principio erat verbum*' the letter *I* is very modest, the *n* is only distinguishable from the rest of the text by the orange dots enclosing it and the rest of the letters are the half-uncial size of the remainder of the text. The letter seems to have been slotted into the small space between the two columns of text, rather than being shown as a major feature of the book.

The stem of the letter '*I*' thickens considerably towards its head, so much so that the illuminator has inserted a white triangle, like the eye of a needle. The bowl of the serif at the head extends into limp wire interlace, with a mosaic of orange-dot infill, yellow shading and unfilled space. The interlace terminates in simple scrolls. The stem narrows considerably towards its base, where it extends into limp wire interlace which also terminates in simple scrolls. It too has some orange-dot infill, some yellow shading and some unfilled mosaic. The stem is outlined in orange dots.

The letter *p*, which is typical of the capitals used in the less significant preface and chapter headings, has the outline of orange dots and also the simple scroll terminals but lacks the mosaic patterns of the initial *I*. However, the cornea-like dots at the ends of the interlace in the scrolls are of note, as are two features on the stem: at the head there is a round 'eye' which breaks up the thickening of the stem and at the foot there is a triangular insert which has a similar effect.

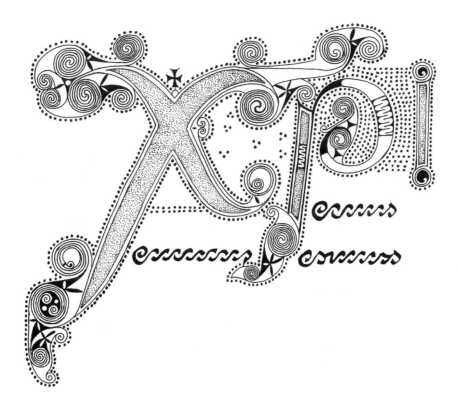

*Chi-Rho initial from*
**The Book of Durrow**
SEVENTH CENTURY,
TRINITY COLLEGE, DUBLIN

# The Chi-Rho Monogram

The initials on the next few pages are the Greek letters Xpi (chi, rho and iota), which together stand for Christ. They usually occur as a fully ornamented page, similar to the major initial pages at the beginning of each Gospel, as the second page or folio of the Gospel according to St Matthew. They mark the beginning of the Christmas story. Only the major Gospel books, such as *The Lindisfarne Gospels*, have the full opening in the form of an initial or capitals:

*Xpi autem generatio sic erat cum esset desponsata mater eius Maria Joseph.*

*(Now the birth of Christ was in this wise when his mother Mary was espoused to Joseph.)*

Clearly the styles of the initials vary considerably, even though the thread of the insular, with its continental derivatives, is common to many of the scriptoria.

The first 'Xpi' comes from an eighth-century insular Gospel. The hollow ground of the *X* is filled with colour, bordered by white, and the stems are curved and taper to a point. They terminate in an, at times, complicated series of spirals. There are single-coil, double-coil and triple-coil spirals, with alternate triquetra, lenses and dots, and concave triangles set in scrolls. The whole of the letter is enclosed by a

single row of red dots. In the top angle of the *X* is a cross on the top of a pole and in the right-hand angle is a scroll. The scroll is an integral part of the border.

The letter *p* is even more complex. The stem is outlined in a thin, black line and has a vellum-coloured outer border enclosing the orange fill of the hollow stem, which is broken in half by a vertical spiral pattern on black. The quill-shaped end of the base has a complex-patterned terminal similar to that of the *X*.

Between the *X* and the *p* the space is filled with triangles of red dots; this may be the illuminator simply using punctuation marks or perhaps a representation of the Holy Trinity. The stem of the *p* has a thin, black ink-line margin, inside of which is a panel shaped like and surrounded by a border which is plain yellow. Within the panel is a short, thick, white, concertinaed line on a black or dark-green background, between two areas of red. The base of the *p* is shaped like the cut point of a quill pen and is extended to form an area within an irregular curvilinear border line, one end of which is pointed while the other is scroll-like. In this area is a single-coil spiral and a larger double-coil spiral, both filled with yellow, between which are a trumpet spiral and lenses of alternate colouring (black and white). The head of the *p* is similarly shaped like a cut pen quill, but the cut is in the opposite direction to that at the base. The ear of the stem extends, in the form of a black horn, into the shoulder of the bowl, where it widens. At the area of greatest width there is a concertina line, similar to that within the stem of the letter but much thicker. After that the bowl then narrows at the loop into another red horn shape, which extends into a lobed single-coil spiral with a yellow background. On either side of this spiral are two small, black, concave-sided triangles. These triangles link the spiral with the border line, which extends to a double-coil spiral, the outer terminal of which is an extended lobe. The counter of the *p* is filled with dark-red dots, which also fill the space between the bowl of the *p* and the letter *i*.

The stem of the letter *i* is similar to that of the *p* but does not have the concertina panel. The terminals are formed of simple spirals with the centres coloured dark red and these are scalloped. The spirals rotate in opposite directions. The letter is enclosed by a row of red dots.

The area of naturally coloured vellum between the letters and the text is filled by regularly spaced S-lines in red.

All of these decorative features are common to many of the insular codices of the seventh and eighth centuries.

*Initial from* **The Corpus Gospels**
EIGHTH CENTURY,
CORPUS CHRISTI COLLEGE, CAMBRIDGE

The Chi-Rho monogram above comes from an eighth-century Irish Gospel. Here the *X* is the only major letter and the continuation letters of the '*PI AUTEM GENERATIO SIC*' are in Irish majuscule, or half-uncial, capitals; the rest of the opening is in the same script as the text – that is, space-saving Irish minuscule script. The *X* is dropped within the text and extends down the left-hand margin for twelve of the thirty-one lines of the page.

The *X* is composed of four curvilinear arms, the centre of each of which has knotted yellow interlace on a plum-coloured background, bordered by a thick yellow line with the outer edge in plum. The two left-hand terminals taper towards their ends, where there are a double-coil spiral, triangular knotted interlace and finally a single-coil spiral. The top right-hand arm's extremity is a double-coil spiral, whereas, in great contrast, the lower right-hand arm terminates in a circle occupied by a face with a rather dour expression. Between these two arms is a mass of spirals, scrolls

*Initial from **The Gospel of St Gatien***
EIGHTH CENTURY, BIBLIOTHÈQUE NATIONALE,
PARIS

and peltas of different colours and combinations of shapes and sizes, including curved triangles and inserted foliage.

The spirals represent the continuous cycle of life, death and rebirth. All are traditional Irish elements going back in an unbroken chain for 500 years. The colours are extremely vivid, with a sparkling yellow, a bright blue and a plum-coloured purple all on a bed of bright red.

The second Chi-Rho shows just about every feature of insular manuscript illumination, except for the human face. Biting bird's heads with exaggerated crests end in single-coil spirals whose bodies are intertwined knotted interlace with lobe endings on a coloured background. The dark colour of the body of the letters is outlined in yellow and each extremity has a yellow 'eye'. One of the terminals of the *X* is a left hand. The stem of the *p* tapers to the base, where it terminates in single-line elbow-knotted interlace with a single-coil spiral ending. At the wider head there is a triangular knotwork insert. The stem bifurcates, with the shoulder of the letter extending into the bowl and loop as a coloured centre with a yellow border. The bowl terminates in the form of an animal head which is biting knotted interlace. The whole of the *Xp* is encompassed by a single line of red dots, but the *i* has been left plain and outside of the array. All of these elements are common to the centres of liturgical book production, especially those in Ireland, between 650 and 1200.

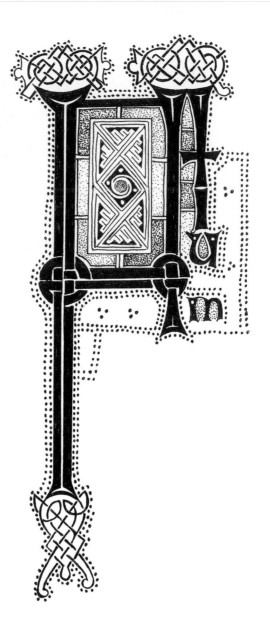

*Initial from* **The Macdurnan Gospels**
NINTH CENTURY, LAMBETH PALACE, LONDON

# The Viking Raids on Armagh

In the late ninth century Armagh was pillaged by the Vikings many times, which indicates that it was a wealthy monastery. However, in the raid of 919 the Vikings plundered the town but spared the churches, the 'Colidei' (the Culdee monastery) and the sick, which suggests some degree of Christianization. Despite the threat of raids, book production continued in the scriptorium and in the last years of the ninth century *The Macdurnan Gospels* were written. It belonged to Maelbrigte, the Abbot of Armagh at the time, who died in 927. It was then brought to England and King Athelstan (924–39) gave it to Canterbury Cathedral, according to the colophon added to the book at the time.

By the eleventh century stability had returned to Armagh and the town and

*Xpi from **Harley MS 1802***
1138, British Library, London

ecclesiastical authorities were subject only to self-inflicted problems. During the early twelfth century there were a number of pocket gospels, roughly six by five inches in size, written in scriptoria in Ireland. Two extant versions were written at Armagh, one of which has in its colophon the name of the scribe, Máel Brigte Ua Máeluánaig, together with notes about historical events dated 1138.

This Gospel has the wire- and ribbon-illuminated initials popular at the time in this scriptorium but the capitals of the text proper are different. The capital shown above is from the beginning of St Matthew's Gospel and is the *X* of the *Xpi*, which is the Chi-Rho monogram of *Christi*, with the *pi* in the body of the text. The *X* extends for nineteen of the twenty-five lines of the page. It is composed of two ribbon-shaped animals, intertwined with a luxuriance of winding foliage with lobed terminals and great flourishes of paws, suggesting the shape of a griffin's wing. The toes have exaggerated nails. The heads of the two animals are turned backwards in order, perhaps, to keep within the margin of the text ruling. They are two-dimensional and thus the viewer sees only the profile of the heads and one foot of each, although the lower head seems to be resting on another paw which belongs to the same animal. The animals have dark-green bodies and the interlace is vellum-coloured. The whole image is drawn on a reddish-orange background.

# Durham A II.10

**O**ne of the earliest insular Gospels, written in the mid-seventh century, contains an elaborate column-length decorative panel of three loops piled one on top of the other as if forming a wing. It is inscribed, in light-red ink, with a colophon marking the end of St Matthew's Gospel (*explicit*) and noting the beginning (*incipit*) of St Mark's, which may have followed on the facing folio. The *explicit* reads:

*Finitum est huius aevangelli secundum Mattheum in nomini domini nostri Iesu Christi nunc incipit aevangelium secundum Marcum in nomine Altissimi amen.*

(Here is finished [the text] of this Gospel according to Matthew in the name of our God Jesus Christ; now begins the Gospel according to Mark in the name of the Most High. Amen.)

The lower panel contains the Paternoster, written in Greek and transliterated into Latin, similar to that in the Book of Armagh, and the early copies of the version of *The Life of St Columba* by Adamnan. The whole of the image fills the right-hand side of a double-columned folio, fourteen and a half by ten and a half inches.

The frame is of yellow interlace with orange-red dots superimposed. The spaces, spandrels, between the bowls of the letters to the right are filled with triangular, or trumpet, knotwork in yellow, orange, green and blue. The outer corners, filled with snake's head pelta ornaments, form a debased Celtic scroll-and-trumpet motif. The counters of the Ds are outlined in thick orange interlace, as are the outer borders on the left side and the top and bottom. The whole feature is a foretaste of what is to come in insular manuscript illumination.

*Decorative panel from* **Durham A.II.10**
EIGHTH CENTURY, DURHAM CATHEDRAL LIBRARY

# Kells Z

This initial is from the most elaborate of all the great illuminated Gospels produced before the eleventh century. Even though the codex was not finished, the skill of the illuminators/artists of the time reached its peak in this great book. The intricate letter above is an initial Z from the beginning of the '*Breves causae*' of St Luke.

A '*Breves causae*', equivalent to the modern chapter, is the summary of each Gospel, but it occurs immediately before rather than at the end of the text. It refers to the numbered divisions of the text, but in this book numbered divisions are absent.

The letter Z, the initial of the word '*Zachariae*', is highly ornamented and decorated. The bowl extends into the two arms of the letter, both panelled, in the form of thick, irregularly knotted interlace in yellow and blue. This has been poorly drawn. A curious feature within this interlace is the three yellow circles, perhaps used to fill the larger gaps left in the uninspired interlace. Above this interlace, in each arm, is a small decorated panel, the same size as the one in the bowl. In the right-hand arm the panel has a diaper pattern of plum and green triangles and in the left-hand arm the infill is like a cross-carpet pattern (all the colours used in the whole letter are included in this small carpet).

The right-hand arm panel contains a large bird in green with yellow interlace extremities, and the left-hand arm contains a peacock with similar yellow interlace

*Part of the continuation lettering from 'Zachariae' in The Book of Kells*
AD 800, TRINITY COLLEGE, DUBLIN

extremities. The cup-like tops of the serifs in both arms have biting animal heads in yellow, with ultramarine bodies and yellow and plum-red interlace extremities. Finally, the counter of the bowl of the letter contains a biting animal head. The tongue of the beast extends as yellow interlace with a lobed terminal. The lower jaw of the beast is being held in the mouth of a peacock, with the rest of the bird filling the counter. Both are drawn on a plum-red background. This is an extremely sumptuous piece of artwork for such a relatively minor part of the Gospel codex.

The asymmetrical bowl of the letter has thick yellow borders, outlined in white and with thin black margins. Within the yellow border are decorated panels. One contains dark-blue interlace, another has a green animal with a yellow biting head and yellow interlace, and another has a larger biting beast in green with yellow interlace. The remaining panel is much smaller and contains a diaper pattern of green and plum-red triangles.

The continuation lettering, which follows the *Z*, is the '*acha*' from *Zachariae* and is in a panel. Unlike the usual simple, angular black letters used elsewhere in the codex as continuation lettering of the lesser initials, these are hollow rounded and enlarged Irish half-uncial forms. The bodies of the first *a* and *h* are ultramarine and those of the *c* and second *a* are orange. All the letters are outlined in yellow and are on a plum-red background. At the end of the panel is a chalice turned on its side, from the mouth of which flow vines in leaf and adorned with grapes. The grapes are being eaten by a beast and a peacock. This perhaps represents the Tree of Life.

# Kells E

**T**his initial is the major capital at the beginning of an ornamental page of text from St Mark's Gospel in an Irish codex. The text, which continues in the usual black angular capitals in a panel with a blue background, reads, '[E]rat autem hora ter[cia]', which translates as 'Now it was the third hour.'

*Initial from* **The Book of Kells**
AD 800, TRINITY COLLEGE, DUBLIN

The ornamentation is similar to that in the *Z* for '*Zachariae*' previously described. The bowl of the letter is divided into panels with thick borders in blue which are outlined in black. The larger panels are filled with yellow elbow knotwork. The three other panels, which are smaller, contain simple key patterns in yellow on a blue background.

The open crossbar of the letter is lens-shaped and contains three panels. The central one is filled with a red-petal cross with dark-blue petals in the angles formed by the arms of the cross, on a yellow background. The panels on either side are the same, each being filled with an interwoven snake with a bud-like terminal to its tail. The Celts believed that the snake, or serpent, was a creature of the underworld which had magical powers because of its knowledge of what happens there concerning the mysteries of death, life and rebirth. It was associated with the lord of the underworld and was not evil in the modern sense at all. The crossbar encloses the inner counter, which is filled with a beast in blue, with a yellow plaited mane and interlace on a red background.

The lower counter is filled with the intertwined bodies in blue of three flat-headed snakes whose 'ears' form yellow elbow interlace and whose tails are tipped with foliage buds, each one in a different pattern. The lower loop of the bowl terminates in the toothed head of a lion. The head is coloured blue and yellow, and part of its mane is in yellow plaited interlace, which extends into the first panel of the bowl. The other part of the mane is made up of a series of blue plate-like scales. The whole letter is an attempt at perpetual motion.

*Initial and continuation lettering opposite above right, 'Fuit homo misus a deo', from* **Durham A.II.10**
EIGHTH CENTURY, DURHAM CATHEDRAL LIBRARY

# The Illuminated Letters

**e**arly book production in the monasteries of Ireland and England was dominated by the writing and illuminating of the great Gospel codices, which were primarily designed for use on the altar and as symbols of the power of God. The decoration of these was focused on five main areas: the canon tables, pictures of the Evangelists, initial pages to each Gospel, carpet or cross-pages and figure subjects. The less emphasized pages, such as the '*argumenta*' and the '*capitula lectionum*', had significantly smaller initials but still had beautiful designs. In the largest of the Gospels some of the other text pages were also regarded with a degree of importance. The initial letter and continuation capitals shown above belong to one of these pandects.

The stem is divided in two and the space between filled with colour but linked by a thin line of interlace. The colours used in this book are mauve, yellow, purple, orange, green and blue green, with black and yellow for the terminals. The left-hand vertical is a continuous black line which narrows towards the head and tail. At the head the line extends into thin knotted interlace, a mosaic filled with colour, and terminates in a bird's head which has a spiral crest. The base of the line shares with the base of the inner upright a pattern, triangular in shape, of thin knotted interlace, with small rings at each of the three points. Both lines extend and terminate in single

spirals with lobed terminals. The crossbar of the letter is hollow and filled with colour; it also terminates in a single spiral. The upper bar likewise terminates in a single spiral but has a concave trumpet serif. Half of the outer counter of the letter is filled with some of the second letter, namely the *U*, and the other half is filled with colour.

The whole of the line of letters, written in thick black ink, reads '*Fuit homo misus a deo*' (saviour of mankind sent by God) and opens the St John the Baptist passage in St John's Gospel. The string of letters, apart from the initial *F*, comprises angular capitals. However, of interest is the misspelling of '*misus*', which should be '*missus*', and the placing vertically of the letters '*do*' (abbreviation of '*deo*'), in order to keep within the prescribed margin of the text, showing that even the scribes and illuminators of these great books could make mistakes.

The whole image flows and is typical of Northumbrian illumination of the eighth century.

*Initial from **Durham A.II.10***
EIGHTH CENTURY, DURHAM CATHEDRAL LIBRARY

# The Cathach

**b**efore the major insular gospel codices of north-west Europe were written, liturgical books in the main originated in Italy and any arriving in the British Isles were brought by missionaries. However, a number of the books produced which are still extant, such as *The Antiphonary of Bangor* and *The Cathach*, display scriptural and artistic features in their illumination which indicate that they were the forerunners of the great books of Durrow and Lindisfarne of the late seventh century. *The Cathach*, which was probably written in the early seventh century, is the earliest surviving Irish psalter (book of psalms); there is a gap of some 400 years before the next group of extant psalters, which were produced from the early eleventh to the thirteenth centuries. *The Cathach* was written in an Irish monastery and is thought to have originally been twice as long as the existing fifty-eight folios, which have been separated and mounted and are now housed with the Royal Irish Academy in Dublin.

Most of the features of the normal Gallican psalters, which originated in Gaul, are present in *The Cathach* (the word *Cathach* means 'battler' and the psalter was carried into battle as a talisman): the psalms follow each other without any division or any emphasis being put on the beginning of a certain psalm by devices such as outsize capitals or a deliberate start at the top of the page.

Each of the sixty-four psalms contained in the psalter has its own large initial. The initials are drawn in black ink with some simple decoration, such as trumpets, spirals or guilloche patterns (ornamental bands or borders with a repeating pattern of two or more interwoven wavy lines). They are often outlined in orange *minium* dots; the headings are also written in orange *minium*. The illumination and the text were probably the work of the same scribe/artist.

*Initials from* The Cathach
AD 591–7, ROYAL IRISH ACADEMY, DUBLIN

Decoration is just one of the features contributed to the text by the scribe/artist. The initials establish two points that are fundamental to later insular book production. First, they are decorated in ways which break up or distort their form; the patterns are not merely fillers or appendages but affect the shape of the letter. Second, the principle of diminution, by which the first initial is larger in size and is followed by other letters which gradually reduce in size until they reach the same size as the script, is established for the first time. The successive narrowing-down of the initial line begins with the first letter.

In *The Cathach* the body of the letter is elastic and mobile. It expands and contracts with a pulsating rhythm. It is this motion that finds expression in the more freely decorative forms in which the stems or curves of the letter end. The closing motif is often a spiral line, which then in turn generates new line formation–trumpet patterns, pelta-like ornament and spherical panels. Sometimes the spiral is replaced by a gaping animal head, a fish perhaps or a porpoise.

Traditionally, *The Cathach* was thought to have been written by St Columba the Elder, who died in 597, though this now seems unlikely. In the medieval legend of his life, it is narrated that he once locked himself in his church at Dromen and there copied a book by St Finnian without having asked permission and, as subsequent events showed, in defiance of his wishes. St Finnian asked for St Columba's copy to be handed over to him, but the latter refused. A judgement in favour of St Finnian eventually led to warlike complications, which culminated in the battle of Cul Dremhne in 561. One of the results of these events was that Columba left Ireland and founded the monastery on Iona. The Columban book at the centre of proceedings is reputed to be preserved in the 'Battle Book' of the O'Donnells, hence the name *Cathach*.

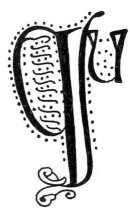

*Initials from* **The Cathach**
AD 591–7, Royal Irish Academy, Dublin

# THE PSALTERS

*Detail from* **The Psalter Ricemarcus**
1079, TRINITY COLLEGE, DUBLIN

# The Psalter Ricemarcus

**I**rish monks had to recite the complete psalter at three different offices every day. This may be why, unlike the early Irish psalters such as *The Cathach of St Columba* (which is the only early extant example), the psalters have three divisions. This division into three 'fifties' (*na trí cóicait*) with the headings of psalms as numbers I, LI and CI treated as the beginnings of each chapter, may be considered as a purely Irish characteristic. At the end of each division there are invariably Collects and Canticles. The beginning of each section is marked by a figured page on one side, usually the verso (the left-hand page, even numbers), and on the opposite side, usually the recto (the right-hand page, odd numbers), a framed page with a large capital, an ornamentation similar to the beginning of the Gospels of the Evangelists we have already seen.

The initials on these pages are similar in style to those used in the insular psalters

*Page from* The Psalter Ricemarcus
1079, TRINITY COLLEGE, DUBLIN

*Detail from* **The Psalter Ricemarcus**
1079, TRINITY COLLEGE, DUBLIN

in the late eleventh century. Here the initial page has a broken border with extremities of the frame formed by animals. The framed border itself is filled with yellow interlace and red-bodied animals with vellum-coloured extremities. The top terminal is in the form of a porpoise, while the lower terminal is made up of the two legs and clawed feet of a beast similar to that of the loop of the capital *Q*. This terminal may be the lower extremity of the beast, while the frame of the border is its body, but it is most unlikely that the porpoise is the head. Here the yellow interlace plaitwork breaks through the body of the creature. The head of the letter is diamond-shaped and at each of the three exposed corners there is a dot and eye feature. The counter of the capital is filled with yellow plaitwork which spills out across the bowl to form elbow knotwork. One terminal of the plaitwork, in the counter, is a biting animal head; the body is the rest of the capital, which terminates as a bowl in the counter of which is the body of a beast with its two legs extending out through the bowl to terminate as clawed feet. The body of the capital is orange. The creatures, other than the porpoise, are very much like seahorses, which must have lived in the warm waters of the Gulf Stream that drifted off the coast of western Britain then as they do today. The letter is enclosed by a single line of red dots and the gaps between the major features are filled with a network of red dots.

The rest of the page is filled with ornamental square capitals.

*David killing the lion from*
***The Southampton Psalter***
ELEVENTH CENTURY,
ST JOHN'S COLLEGE,
CAMBRIDGE

# The Southampton Psalter

The *Southampton Psalter* is a good example to take of this sort of work. Here the tripartite divisions occur as follows:

Folio 4v:     full-page illumination – David killing lion;

Folio 5r:     introductory page to the first 'fifty' – '*Beatus vir*';

Folio 38v:    crucifixion;

Folio 39r:    introductory page to second 'fifty' – '*Quid gloriaris*'

Folio 68v:    David and Goliath;

Folio 69r:    introductory page the third 'fifty' – '*Domine exaudi*'.

*Initial page from*
**The Southampton Psalter**
ELEVENTH CENTURY,
ST JOHN'S COLLEGE, CAMBRIDGE

Besides the heavily ornamented pages of miniatures and initials, the psalters contain many smaller initials. The initials opposite are two examples of the style used in this group of Irish psalters from the eleventh and twelfth centuries. Each initial usually introduces a psalm, is often drawn slightly indented into the text line and commonly extends down the left-hand margin of the page for at least four or five lines. Each text page, measuring approximately ten by seven inches, has thirty to thirty-two single lines of half-uncial script.

The initials on the opposite page are representative of the two styles of minor initials used in the psalter: ribbon animal and knotted-wire. These are often alternated through most of the psalter in what seems to be a deliberate fashion. The ribbon initial is a close relation of the animals on the large initial introductory pages, having all the same characteristics, including the curved claws. The body of the animal is a thick, mauve-coloured ribbon which tapers into one leg with a long, clawed-foot terminal. The other terminal is the head of the animal which has a passive mouth, the lower jaw of which has been extended as the yellow border for the whole of the body of the letter. Also on the head of the beast is an extended spiral crest with a lobed terminal, which is different from those examples used in the seventh- and eighth-century Irish manuscripts. The counter of the letter is filled with thick, yellow plaitwork, like basketry, which breaks

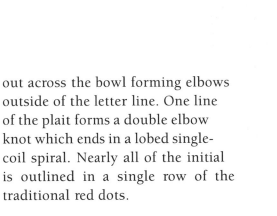

out across the bowl forming elbows outside of the letter line. One line of the plait forms a double elbow knot which ends in a lobed single-coil spiral. Nearly all of the initial is outlined in a single row of the traditional red dots.

The bodies of the two animals in the wire initial are much slimmer than those in the ribbon-initial animal. The heads are similar but each has an ear rather than an extended crest and the tails are very different. The stem-like animal's tail is thinner and ends in a single-coil spiral, as if curled like a cat's. The other animal's body is much longer and half-way along its length it is elbow-knotted round the body of the other. The half towards the head forms the bowl of the initial, while the other half tapers to form the tail, which is shaped like a bell. The bell has colour infill and two three-ring terminals. The counter of the letter has a colour infill with three large double-line interlocking rings, which have a different colour infill from the counter. The whole of the initial, except the bell, is outlined with a single row of red dots.

The colours used are yellow, orange and mauve but no green.

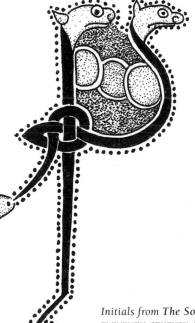

*Initials from **The Southampton Psalter***
ELEVENTH CENTURY, ST JOHN'S COLLEGE, CAMBRIDGE

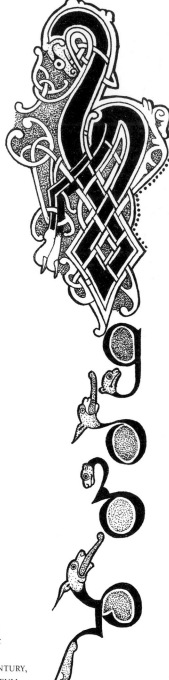

*Initials from*
*The Cormac*
*Psalter*
TWELFTH CENTURY,
BRITISH MUSEUM,
LONDON

# The Cormac Psalter

The initials are from a Gallican psalter, written in the mid-twelfth century in a monastery in Ireland by a scribe named Cormac. This is known because the scribe has signed his name, '*Cormacus scripsit hoc psalterium ora pro eo. Qui legis hoc ora pro sese qualibet hora*', in the colophon at the end of the first 'fifty' division of the psalter.

The quality of the illumination in the psalter is very good. The initials illustrated here are from one of the ordinary text pages, which indicates the high standard of the major initial pages at the beginning of the psalms. Our initial and its attendant capitals which open each verse glow with intense shades of blue, purple, green and yellow. It is a letter *B* of the ribbon style of initial. The elongated body and legs are purple in colour, with the diamond-shaped lower section in intense green. The clawed feet and the horse-like head are the colour of the vellum, which has aged to a yellowish white. The intertwined tendrils of the foliage are bright yellow. They often terminate in a yellow lobe and one has broken out into a leaf. The leaf buds have been coloured red. The whole of the initial is on an orange-red background. Usually the initial would have been outlined with a single row of orange-red dots, but here only a small length has been dotted.

The accompanying capitals which open the verses are very similar to those of the majestic *Book of Kells*, the peak of Irish illumination. All the letters are in black ink and the counters are coloured. The first letter immediately below the initial *B* is a *Q* with the stem terminating in a typical Irish dog-head zoomorph. The next letter down, *D*, has a stem terminal of a dog with a gaping mouth and a thick, protruding tongue. The next letter is also a *D*, but the illuminator has varied it by adding

*Page from* **The Cormac Psalter**

a triangle to the line of the ascender. The last letter is a *P*, the ascender of which ends again in a dog-head terminal with a gaping mouth and thick, protruding tongue. The descender terminal ends in the foot and claw of the animal. Both ascender and descender are curved outwards, in order, perhaps, to maintain the symmetry.

The capitals increase in size towards the bottom of the page. All the letters, which run down the whole length of the page, are outside the ruling margin of the text. The script is twenty lines of Irish half-uncial on a page about seven by five inches. The psalter, which contains 179 folios, shows that the traditional forms of Irish illumination, originating some 300 years earlier, had not been lost despite the Viking incursions.

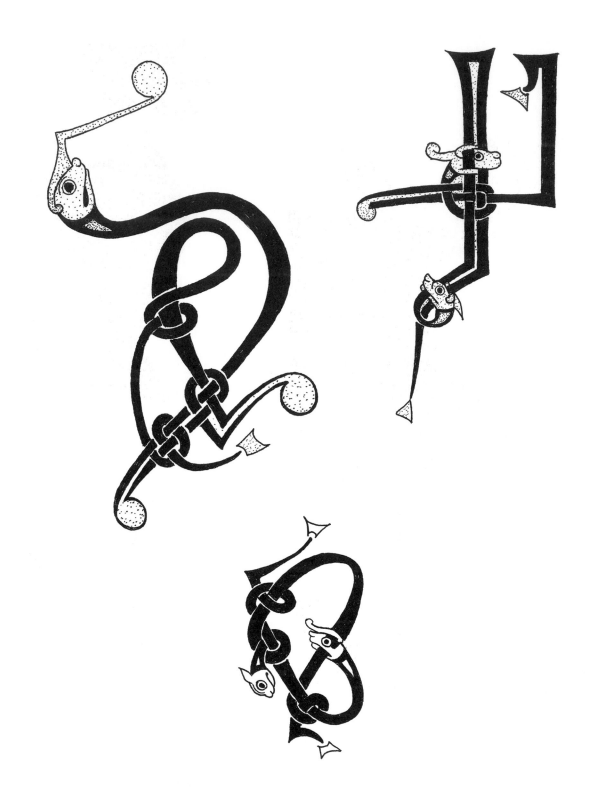

*Initials from* **The St Ouen Psalter**
TENTH CENTURY, BIBLIOTHÈQUE MUNICIPALE, ROUEN

*Initials from* The Psalter of St Caimin
ELEVENTH CENTURY, FRANCISCAN HOUSE, KILLINEY

*Initial from* **The Corpus Missal**
TWELFTH CENTURY, CORPUS CHRISTI COLLEGE, OXFORD

# The Corpus Missal

The initial above is from an Irish missal, written around 1120, that is very lavishly decorated, although only the capitals are ornamented. A missal is a service book containing the texts necessary for the performance of the mass and includes chants, prayers and readings, together with ceremonial directions. Principal fields for decoration are the canon page, with the text '*Te igitur*', and the '*Vere dignum*' monogram.

The capitals, which appear on nearly every page, are very large for the size of the book page, which is six and three-quarters by four and three-quarters inches. They incorporate features of a Scandinavian style of ornament, with emphasis being given to wide-ribboned bodies of beasts, in contrast to the thin-bodied network of snakes which gives a general rhythm to the composition based on sinuous lines. However, the head of the beast on the capital above is not the flattened head of Scandinavian monsters but the sturdy, active, barking and biting head of the traditional Irish initials.

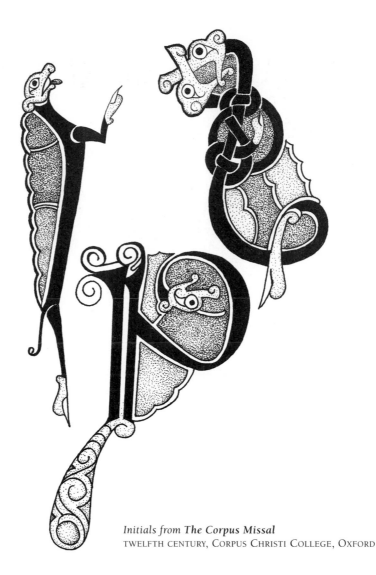

*Initials from* **The Corpus Missal**
TWELFTH CENTURY, CORPUS CHRISTI COLLEGE, OXFORD

The bright ribbon beast drawn in profile is coloured purple and has gaping jaws and toes with extended nails. The bodies of snakes, formed from thick yellow interlace, are intertwined with the body of the beast. The bodies terminate at one end in flat snake's heads and at the other end in a lobed tail.

This style of initial is sometimes referred to as Urnes, because the bodies of the beasts are similar to carvings on the church at Urnes in Norway and date from the same period. As the snake was believed to regain its youth with the shedding of its skin, it symbolizes Christ's resurrection.

The whole of the initial is on a red field and projects well into the line of the text, which is written in Irish miniscule script. It typifies the style of illumination adopted by some of the Irish scriptoria, such as those at Glendalough and Clonmacnois, well after the warlike Scandinavian incursions had ceased and the intruders had settled in Ireland.

*Initial from D.II.3*
EIGHTH CENTURY,
ROYAL IRISH ACADEMY,
DUBLIN

# Sacramentary

A sacramentary is a service book containing the prayers recited by the celebrant during high mass: the collect, post-communion and the canon of the mass. The other parts of the mass are contained in the evangelary, the epistolary and the gradual. The texts of the sacramentary are divided into the unchanging elements, the canon and the ordinary of the mass, and the vari-able texts, the latter arranged according to the liturgical year. Further divisions are the common of saints (standard formulas for saints who are not accorded individual services) and votive masses for special occasions, such as marriage.

The sacramentary was replaced by the missal during the eighth century. As we have seen, the missal is a service book containing the texts necessary for the performance of the mass. Its development was prompted by the custom of saying private masses and low masses which were performed by the celebrant alone.

The initial letter opposite comes from an Irish sacramentary/missal of the eighth century. It is the '*IN P*' of the '*In principio*' which marks opening of the Gospel of St John. The initial occupies at least 60 per cent of the available page area, inside the decorated border, with the remainder containing the text written in Irish minuscule script. What would be a very thick, black-ink stem of the combination of the capital *I* and the left-hand upright of the *N* has been reduced by tapering the stem almost to a point. Also the two components are separated by a thick line of uncoloured vellum which reduces the heaviness of the stem. The tapering base has a terminal of black single-line interlace, on coloured ground, which is extended as the necks of two animals. The heads of the two beasts have protruding thin tongues; at the end of one are grapes and the other a single fruit. The two ears at the head of the combined stem extend into black-line interlace, which becomes the heads of two similar beasts which do not have protruding tongues. At the other end of the bodies, the interlace terminates in lobes.

The bar of the *N* is a single, thick black line which ends at the right-hand, upright of the letter. This upright is separated from the stem of the *P* by a thick vellum line. The shortness of the stems obviates the need for tapering. At their base is a single black-line knotted interlace with lobed terminals on coloured ground. At their head the ears of the stems extend into single black-line knotted interlace with beasts' heads, which is the same as the other terminal. The shoulder of the letter *P* extends into the bowl, which is drawn down and joins the stem two-thirds of the way along its length. Curiously, at this point another bowl is drawn out, which curls back on itself to form an open counter in which there is a feature like an apple with a bite taken out of it. This curled leg or tail is purely decorative, as the letter *r* of the '*principio*' is written in the text.

Between the two stems of the *N* there are mosaic patterns. The larger, which is quartered and fills the whole area with contrasting colours, encompasses the smaller, which is filled with a fretwork design. The colours used by the illuminator are yellow, orange and brownish red. Of interest is the total absence of dots.

*Initial from* **Codex 213**
EIGHTH CENTURY, DOMBIBLIOTHEK, COLOGNE

# Canons

Canons are Church decrees enacted to regulate morals or religious practices or ecclesiastical laws based on the rulings of the early Church councils.

The initials shown above and on the facing page are included in a manuscript which was written and illuminated to the same standard as the luxury Gospel codices of the early eighth century. It was clearly designed to impress, as were the altar books and some missionary texts. This codex was illuminated in Lindisfarne and sent from England to the Continent during the eighth century, probably reaching Cologne by around 800. It is likely that it was commissioned for missionary purposes. At the end of the manuscript the words '*Sigibertus scripsit*' appear, as they do in a companion book, Codex 212. Sigibertus was an eighth-century scribe at Cologne, where the book has remained ever since.

The early part of the 143-folio text includes a series of five minor initial letters which incorporate both bird and geometric ornaments. The initials have a turning-bird design with interlace panels within the double-pencil-style drawing of the body and neck. The legs, body and neck of the bird have been drawn out to meet the design, which was copied later in insular and Romanesque art. Coloration was limited to orange, yellow and green, and the text was written in insular majuscule.

The bird is a symbol of spirituality. Different sorts of bird were illustrated by particular artists. Those in the Lindisfarne liturgical books, for example, were most probably cormorants, which are local to that area.

*Initial from* **Codex 213**
EIGHTH CENTURY, DOMBIBLIOTHEK, COLOGNE

## The Liber Hymnorum

The capital shown here is from an early-eleventh-century hymnal. A hymnal, also called a hymnary, contains metrical hymns sung in the divine office which are arranged according to the liturgical year. The hymnal was often contained, as a separate section, within a psalter or antiphonal. Later its contents were incorporated into the breviary, which collected all the components of the divine office which the cleric had to recite during the day.

Our hymnal, which is a collection of hymns in Latin and Irish, was probably meant for choir use, as the features are large enough to be seen by a number of people at the same time. It is similar to a number of other manuscripts from this period, all of which probably had a common exemplar.

Each hymn starts with a large, ornamental initial which is extremely elaborate, and the verses have a small capital filled with colour. The colours used were brilliant green, red, yellow and purple. The coloration continually varies from one small initial to the next, and from page to page.

The large, ornamental initials are of two types. The first, illustrated on the page opposite and the most commonly used, is the ribbon, which is curvilinear in pattern; the second is the more traditional, dominant straight-line type. In the former, the foliage ornament, in yellow, in inextricably mixed with the animals and threads like knots backwards and forwards, eventually enlarging at the end into a suggestion of a curled leaf. These scrolling tendrils, which break into leaf ends and lobed foliage, are like acanthus and may have derived from it. The animals themselves constitute the ribbon letters, and purple is often used to colour between the two thick black parallel lines of their margin. In the latter, the artist used an elaborate system of dots, some surrounding the letter in the traditional fashion and others superimposed, either in black ink or the other colours used, such as red or yellow on purple, green on yellow or purple on red. The elongated animals have straight-line bodies, together with the other features of traditional Irish zoomorphology.

This style of lettering has been called Ringerike, which is a Scandinavian style of the early eleventh century characterized by loose and sometime ragged foliate scrolls and interlacings with acanthus motifs. Used by Scandinavian metalworkers, it was modified by Irish metalworkers to include zoomorphic features.

*Detail from*
***The Liber Hymnorum***
ELEVENTH CENTURY,
TRINITY COLLEGE, DUBLIN

*Initial from B10.5*
TRINITY COLLEGE, CAMBRIDGE

# Trinity P

This initial comes from an eighth-century *Epistulae S Pauli* which was written in England, probably by an Irish scribe. An epistolary is a service book containing the epistle readings for the mass, arranged according to the liturgical year. These readings are generally taken from the New Testament Epistles, but are sometimes drawn from other New and Old Testament books. At high mass the epistle was read by the subdeacon (the priest who celebrated the mass was assisted by a deacon, who in turn was assisted by a subdeacon).

The initial *P* is drawn in black ink. The slender stem tapers to the base, where it curves as an extended outward hairline serif. On the upper surface of the serif there is a hollow triangle, filled with yellow and a single red dot. The triangle is similar to an abbreviated uncial letter *a*. The head of the stem is wider than the base and forms a bowl, with the left margin extending as a short ear. The right margin becomes the bowl of the letter. At its beginning it is a thick, black line, but it then widens at the bow to become hollow, the hollow being filled with yellow paint and a single line of red dots. The bowl then narrows at the loop and continues as a thick, black line until it reaches the terminal. The terminal is in the form of a hollow isosceles triangle filled with yellow paint; a smaller triangle contains a red dot. The angles of the triangle extend as finials and one continues as red dots into the counter of the letter.

The counter of the *P* contains triangular groups of three red dots, which may represent the Holy Trinity, and a letter *a* in the half-uncial form with its counter filled with yellow paint. Also there is a half-uncial form of the letter *u* and the word '*dicimis*' is written in half-uncial script. These letters form, with the letter '*lus*' outside of the capital, the phrase '*Paulus dicimis*', which means 'Paul speaks.' The whole of the letter is enclosed by a single row of red dots.

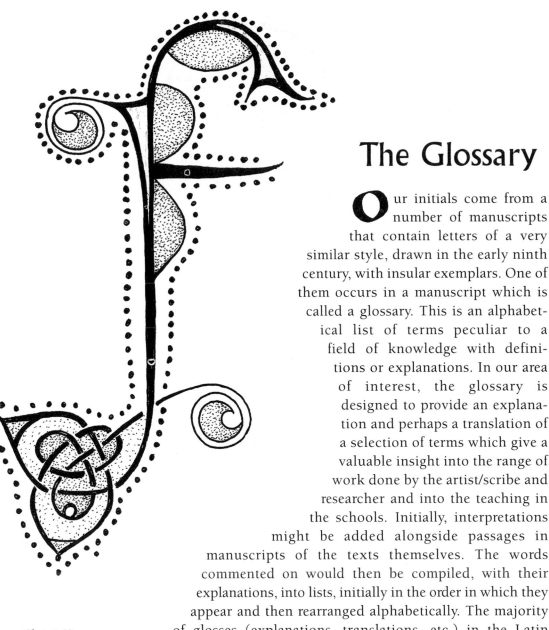

*Initial from* **Corpus Christi 69**
NINTH CENTURY,
CORPUS CHRISTI COLLEGE, CAMBRIDGE

# The Glossary

Our initials come from a number of manuscripts that contain letters of a very similar style, drawn in the early ninth century, with insular exemplars. One of them occurs in a manuscript which is called a glossary. This is an alphabetical list of terms peculiar to a field of knowledge with definitions or explanations. In our area of interest, the glossary is designed to provide an explanation and perhaps a translation of a selection of terms which give a valuable insight into the range of work done by the artist/scribe and researcher and into the teaching in the schools. Initially, interpretations might be added alongside passages in manuscripts of the texts themselves. The words commented on would then be compiled, with their explanations, into lists, initially in the order in which they appear and then rearranged alphabetically. The majority of glosses (explanations, translations, etc.) in the Latin glossaries were in Latin but there were also several in Old English. For example, one glossary gave a short alphabetical dealing with words of Greek and Hebrew origin.

The style and decoration of these manuscripts were not very exotic and certainly did not match the degree of ornamentation used in the great Gospels. However, the manuscripts were still regarded as being of importance, especially in the scholastic field, and some illumination was used. As they were produced in the monastic scriptoria, the scribes and illuminators had access to all the design features of other liturgical books.

The initial F on the previous page has a slender stem, drawn in black ink, extending at the base into interlace patterns, like elbow knotwork, on a coloured background,

with the terminal being a single simple scroll with scalloped colour infill. The colours used in the manuscript are yellow, green, blue and pale red. The stem thickens towards its head and to avoid what would be a top-heavy feel the illuminator has included a white elongated 'eye', turning the stem into the sort of needle used in sewing. The two arms of the letter are balanced by a scroll-like extension on the opposite side of the stem, similar to that of the terminal at the base. The lower arm is a short, tapering thick line of black ink, while the upper arm is curved, forming a half-bowl. The arm has a white insert similar to that in the head of the stem and ends in an asymmetrical concave serif. The whole of the letter is enclosed in a continuous line of red dots, as is the custom with insular illumination. Lastly, there is one unusual feature: the half-bowls of colour which occur at three points along the right-hand side of the stem. These are perhaps buttresses, often used to strengthen the slender stems.

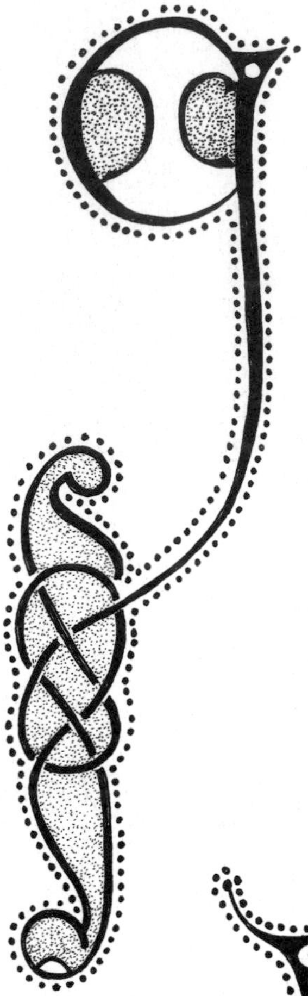

The *Q* has many similar features to the *F*, but additions are the 'bull's-eye' and the 'ear' balancing the shoulder at the head of the stem.

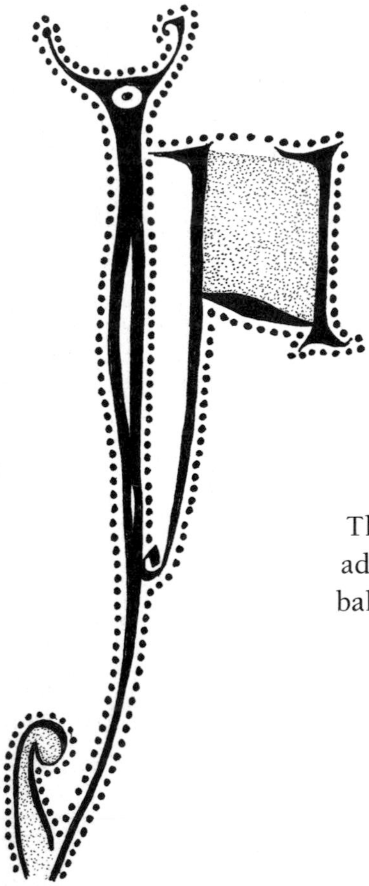

*Initials from*
**Corpus Christi 69**
NINTH CENTURY,
CORPUS CHRISTI COLLEGE,
CAMBRIDGE

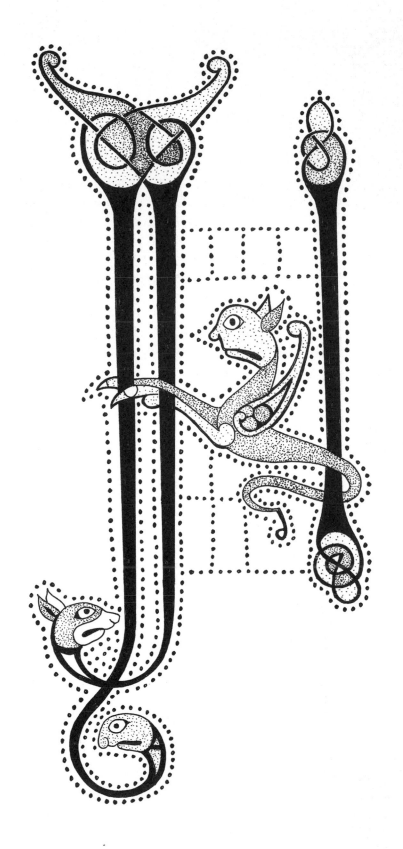

*Initial from* **The Royal Prayerbook**
NINTH CENTURY, BRITISH LIBRARY, LONDON

*Initial from The Royal Prayerbook*
NINTH CENTURY, BRITISH LIBRARY, LONDON

# The Royal Prayerbook

The monogram initial *IN*, in bold black on the previous page, introduces a prayer in the ninth-century *Royal Prayerbook*. This manuscript belongs to a group of insular devotional texts around a central theme such as Christ the healer. The text plays on an image which equates the Godhead with the physician or *medicus* of man, for whom corporeal disease is the emblem of his sinful nature. Prayers regularly talk of Christ as the sinners' doctor.

Both the text, in minuscule, and the illumination, especially the extensive use of reddish-orange dots, exhibit an Irish influence. The initial extends for seven of the eighteen lines of the page.

The slender stem of the *I* tapers to its base, where it terminates in an earless, passive animal head which is the colour of the vellum. Along with the left-hand upright of the letter *N*, the *I* terminates at its head in a mosaic formed by the single black-line interlace which is the continuation of the finials of the cup-like serifs. The colours added to the natural colour of the vellum are reddish orange and green. The left-hand slender stem of the letter *N* tapers towards its base, where it terminates in a passive animal head coloured reddish orange and green. This animal head is in profile and has two offset ears. The slender right-hand stem of the *N* widens at both head and base, where it ends in a mosaic of black-line interlace with green and orange-red sectors. The bar of the *N* is a mythical winged two-legged creature, seen in profile, with a passive head, clawed front legs and a tapering body with a long, narrow tail ending in a lobe.

The letters are enclosed by a single line of reddish-orange dots and between the stems of the *N*, where the field is not filled with the animal, there is a rectangular pattern of red dots.

It is called *The Royal Prayerbook* because it is in the royal collection of the British Library in London. This collection, the personal property of the sovereigns of England, was started by Edward IV in the fifteenth century.

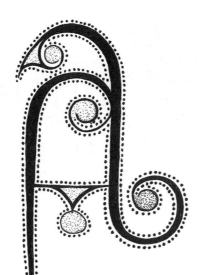

*Initial from*
***The Book of Nunnaminster***
EIGHTH CENTURY,
BRITISH LIBRARY, LONDON

# The Book of Nunnaminster

The three initials illustrated here and on the following page are the only significant capitals in a mid-eighth-century book of prayers, a *Libellus Precum*, which probably belonged to a woman, as the flyleaves at the back of the book carry a prayer in a late-ninth-century hand of feminine form. It was intended as a programme of private devotion arranged around the central theme of meditation upon the life of Christ. It begins with extracts from the life of Christ, followed by a medley of devotional texts, most of them prayers, which are thanksgiving for Christ's passion. It probably belonged to Ealhswith, wife of King Alfred, and to St Mary's Abbey, Winchester (Nunnaminster), which was founded by her.

The initials demonstrate the kinds of capitals and ornamentation the Anglo-Saxon illuminators had available as exemplars when book production resumed after the interruptions of the ninth-century invasions from Scandinavia. These are probably from Northumbrian models. They are in black ink, sparingly coloured with orange and green and enclosed by either single or double rows of orange-red dots.

The initial *A* is a graceful series of curves linked by stems in black ink. Each curve tapers to its extremity, where it forms a simple hook on a red or green background. The capital has two isosceles triangles filled with colour. The tapering descender extends as single black-line interlace, which forms a mosaic with reddish and green sectors. It is typical of the insular style for the capital letter *A*.

The *D* (overleaf top left) is the same style as the *A*. Its black-ink bowl thickens at

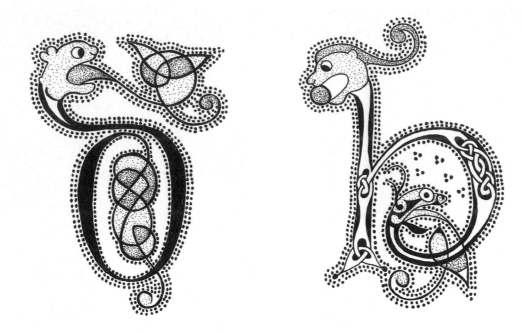

*Initials from The Book of Nunnaminster*
EIGHTH CENTURY, BRITISH LIBRARY, LONDON

the sides and has narrow loops at the top and bottom. The upper loop of the bowl extends into the counter as black single-line interlace and has broken through the lower loop to end in a simple hook. The single-line interlace forms a mosaic of red, green and the vellum colour. The right side of the bow extends by bending back over the counter – a typical uncial style of the letter *D* – and terminates in an animal head drawn in profile, occupying the serif. The animal head has two ears showing, even though it is seen from the side. In its gaping mouth is a reddish, thickened tongue which is extended as black, intertwined single-line interlace, which forms a mosaic similar to that in the counter. The interlace terminates as a hook on a green background. The whole feature is enclosed by a double row of red-orange dots.

Whereas the *D* top right and the *A* from the previous page are clearly in the same style and originate from the same exemplar, the initial *H* is very different and was probably copied from a different exemplar. The stem is drawn in white on a black background. At one point it has an integral knot, a string of which extends to form the bowl of the letter, and where it thickens there is a more complex series of integral knots. These also are drawn in white on a black background. The bow terminates in a gaping beast's head, with a thickened tongue narrowing to form single-line interlace as it breaks out of and into the counter through the bowl. Within the counter there are triangular groups of three dots, which may relate to the Holy Trinity. The head of the stem is formed by a beast's head with a toothless gaping mouth in which has been placed a round object. The mane of the beast, which is filled with colour, extends and narrows, ending in a lobe. The whole initial is enclosed by a double row of reddish-orange dots.

# NON-LITURGICAL MANUSCRIPTS

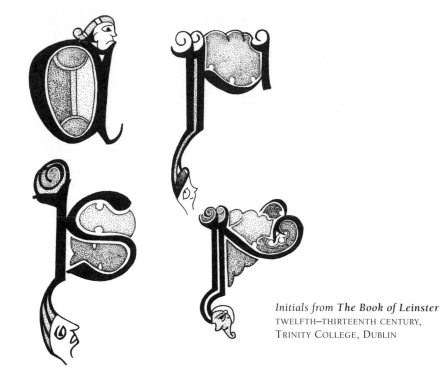

*Initials from* **The Book of Leinster**
TWELFTH–THIRTEENTH CENTURY,
TRINITY COLLEGE, DUBLIN

# The Book of Leinster

This group of initials comes from an Irish manuscript dating from the late twelfth century which is a collection of early Irish sagas and genealogies. It was written by an abbot of the monastery at Terryglass, as evidenced by the statement, 'Áed Húa Crimthaind wrote this book and collected it from many books.' Aed was abbot after 1152, so the manuscript must have been started around that date and was added to into the first quarter of the thirteenth century, when Aed died. Parts of it were probably written in other places which were the actual sources of the information.

There is only one major initial in the book, but the many minor initials are exemplified by the group shown above. The stems and bows of the capitals, in thick black ink, are the usual wire initials but are thicker in outline and include many different shapes of margin. The counters are filled with mosaics of colour drawn from the usual combinations for Irish manuscripts of this period: mauve, orangy red, yellow and

*Detail from **The Barberini Gospels***
AD 750, VATICAN LIBRARY, ROME

green. The usual forms of spirals, serifs and tails are also present. However, the scribe/artist surpassed himself in the use of caricatural human profiles as the terminals of the stems of the letters. Like the rest of the decoration, they are on a small scale but are drawn with a delicately light, hardly scratched touch of a pen. They are unlike those in the earlier *Book of Kells* and others of continental origin, for the foliation and other impedimenta have been discarded and, as a result by their isolation, the heads have been given a sharper definition and an acutely individual character. This feature makes the manuscript unique among the insular books extant prior to the twelfth century.

The chaotic situation in England during much of the ninth century, with the consequent decline of culture, explains why it was impossible to produce many decorated manuscripts of good quality. For 100 years the Scandinavian incursions interrupted monastic life. As a result, the monks at Lindisfarne were finally forced to abandon the monastery complex in 876, as had the clerics at the Monkwearmouth and Jarrow sites the year before. It was not until the end of the century that ornamented initials began to appear again, and when they did they were not of the same quality as the great initial pages of illumination in the Gospels from the major scriptoria in the eighth and ninth centuries. However, their importance lies in the fact that they are a bridge between the highly productive period up to the early ninth century and the similarly productive tenth and eleventh centuries in England. They show that the art of illuminating manuscripts, which had been put on the

*Initial from Ovid's **Ars Amatoria**, Book I*
NINTH CENTURY, BODLEIAN LIBRARY, OXFORD

back shelf, was ready to be dusted off and could now be practised again for the greater glory of God.

A good example is provided by the ten extant folios of the late-ninth-century manuscript of Ovid's *Ars amatoria*, Book 1, which was produced in Wales (Wales was most probably not greatly affected during the upheavals elsewhere in Britain at that time) and was in possession of Glastonbury Abbey by the middle of the tenth century. Its initials are the direct descendants of the small capitals found in manuscripts such as the late-eighth-century *Barberini Gospels*.

The manuscript gives us the monogram *Si*, although it is not easy to distinguish the two letters. The decoration is composed of a series of animal's and bird's heads arranged down the stems of the letters and at the terminals, forming a continuous pattern. Along the stems there are two bird's heads which bite the stems and two animal's heads with extended crest-like features which are lobe-ended and similar to the beaks of the birds. The stem terminals are a variety of animal's heads, with the base one being extended into a leg and paw that are decorated with bands of colour. The terminal at the head of the letter *i* is a plan view of one of these heads which has the appearance of having been flattened. The monogram is drawn in black ink and it extends down the left-hand margin of the text for thirteen of the thirty-three lines of the page, the text of which is written in a Welsh variety of Anglo-Saxon minuscule script.

The initial on this page comes from the books *Ars Amatoria* (*The Art of Love*) by Ovid (Publius Ovidius Naso), who was born near Rome in 43 BC. He was destined to become a great orator but chose instead the life of a poet. The contents of *Ars Amatoria* and a love affair with the granddaughter of the emperor Augustus were contributory factors to his – and her – banishment from Rome.

# Orosius

These capitals come from an early-seventh-century manuscript which is a copy of the *Chronicon* of Orosius. Paulus Orosius was born and lived in Spain in the fifth century. He was a pupil of Augustine, who encouraged him to write a Christian chronicle, the *Historiae Adversum Paganos*. Written in seven books, this was an account of the history of the world from the creation to the founding of Rome and its history up to 417. Orosius drew from many non-Christian sources for his text, including such Roman authors as Livy and Tacitus.

The first folio of this early-seventh-century copy contains the earliest-known carpet page of insular art. Our capitals are on folio two and form the words '*PRAECEPTIS TUIS PA*' with the '*RUI*' of the word '*parui*' on the next line. All the capitals are hollow-shafted and the shafts are filled with pink or orange. Each capital is likely to have been drawn without the aid of instruments, because the lines that should be straight are irregular, as if done with a shaking hand. Perhaps the scribe used an extremely fine-pointed instrument which was difficult to control. The drawn-out stem of the letter *P* runs the whole length of the written area of the page, some seven inches, and is outside of the text; in fact, it acts as a margin for the twenty-one lines of half-uncial text. The bowl of the letter projects into the line of the text and is joined to the stem by means of a form of hook-and-eye. The stem and the bowl have a cable pattern reversed in white. There are rows of orange dots in the counter and also in the space below the bowl. Triple dots, in the form of triangles, occur in the counter of the letter *R* and may represent the Holy Trinity.

This use of pattern and colour, together with the inclusion of dots, is typical of the work of insular scribes and illuminators of the seventh century. The head of the stem is flat with no ornamentation, whereas the base has a square drawn within a square

and an *x* drawn through both squares. The curious feature which terminates the stem is possibly a form of serif, as the other letters include hairline, tick and rolled serifs, or perhaps it is a French crochet hook. It was included to strengthen the drawn-out stem of the letter. All the letters are similar to those in *The Cathach of St Columba*.

*The Soul*

*I am a flame of fire, blazing with passionate love;*
*I am a spark of light, illuminating the deepest truth.*

*Extract from **The Black Book of Camarthen***

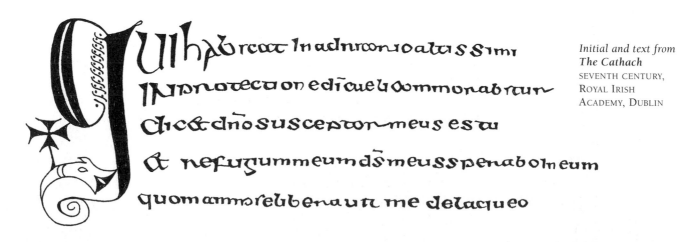

*Decorative script from Bede's Historia Ecclesiastica Gentis Anglorum*
EIGHTH CENTURY, BRITISH LIBRARY, LONDON

# The Venerable Bede

**b**ede was born in 673 when the conversion of England, begun by St Augustine of Canterbury around 600, was reaching completion. He created forty-five books and in 731 completed his major work, *Historia Ecclesiastica Gentis Anglorum* (*Ecclesiastical History of the English People*), shortly before his death in 735.

> *I, Bede, servant of Christ and priest of the Abbey of St Peter and St Paul at Wearmouth and Jarrow, have compiled this history, with the help of God, using for it old documents, ancient traditions and what I have been able to see with my own eyes. Born in the neighbourhood of the said monastery, I was only seven years old, when my parents confided me to the care of Abbot Benedict [Biscop]. Since then I have passed my whole life in the cloister, dividing my time between the study of Holy Writ and regular and daily observance of the Holy Office. My whole happiness was in studying, teaching and writing. I was ordained a deacon at nineteen, and priest at thirty, these two orders being conferred on me by Bishop John of Beverly. Since I became a priest to the present time, when I have reached the age of fifty-nine, I have employed my time in writing, for my own use and that of all my brothers, commentaries on the Holy Scripture, sometimes taken from the Holy Fathers, sometimes conceived in their spirit and according to their interpretation.*

The enlarged decorated display capitals shown opposite are a copy from Book II of the *Ecclesiastical History* and occupy a separate area of the page from the text. However, they are not panelled, panelling being the usual style of the openings in the rest of this manuscript and its relatives, such as *The Book of Cerne*. The capital letter *H* has a hollow stem, bowl and leg which are filled with knotwork in yellow drawn on a

*Initial from Bede's **Historia Ecclesiastica Gentis Anglorum***
EIGHTH CENTURY, BRITISH LIBRARY, LONDON

black background. Sets of knots are linked by circles of colour infill. The head of the stem has single-line knotwork which is filled with background colour and its base is formed of a simple scroll, as is the base of the leg. All of the letter, except the outer counter, is enclosed by a continuous single row of orange-coloured dots. The outer counter is filled with a bird on a plant scroll, with a coloured background and a frame of the vellum colour.

The continuation lettering is drawn in black ink and is in the form of enlarged display capitals embellished with zoomorphic ornament, but unlike the legends in the other books it is not panelled. Some of the letters have zoomorphic features, such as earless and biting animal-head terminals. There is a face in profile in the counter of the *t*. The counters are usually filled with colour, either yellow, orange or green.

# Priscian

The enlarged capital letter *P* is dropped in the text, with the left side in line with the left margin, and the zoomorphic decoration at the top of the bow extends above the top of the text line. The letter extends down for ten lines of the text and the equivalent of three lines above the top line of the text. The text is written in Latin and the script is Irish minuscule.

The style of the letters of which the *P* is an example belongs to the mid-ninth-century manuscripts of Ireland, especially those from the scriptorium of the monastery at Armagh. The outline of the letter is drawn in black ink. The bowl of the letter terminates at one end in a beast's head, with its mouth biting the left foot of the human figure, and extends as the body of the animal through the stem of the letter to another beast-head terminal at the other end. Here the beast's head is not gaping, but the ears are extended into elbowed interlace.

Returning to the inner counter, we find the central feature is an elongated human figure whose hands are holding the bowl, while another part of its circumference is held between the figure's calf and thigh muscles as it sits cross-legged. The chin of the head of the figure is resting on the outer rim of the bowl and the large eyes stare forwards. The chin is beardless, which suggests the figure may be a representation of a youthful Christ. The head does not have a mouth but has an Irish tonsure, with the remaining hair extending down on either side over the bowl and into the counter, where it is then wrapped around the bowl in the form of elbowed interlace. The attitude of the figure is one of prayer or supplication. On either side of the figure, both within the counter and extending outside of it, are two inward-facing birds. The rear-extending parts of the bird's crests are represented by knotted and elbowed interlace and the forward-extending parts end in a lobe. A wing of the left-hand-side bird extends between the double-lined shaft of the capital and out of the letter, where it terminates in a single spiral with paired lenses. This spiral is scrolled, with two double spirals, and the space in between is occupied by three lenses forming a triangular pattern. The spirals seem to maintain the symmetry of the counter and bowl of the letter. The spiral within the wing of the bird may be an 'eye', which would suggest that the birds are peacocks, symbols of the incorruptibility of Christ since the peacock's flesh was said not to putrefy.

The letter begins the text of the second page of a 120-folio grammatical textbook, called a Priscian after its author, Priscian, or more correctly Priscianus Caesariensis, who was a sixth-century Italian Latin grammarian who taught in Constantinople and wrote many texts, including this *Institutiones Grammaticae*, which had a profound influence on the teaching of Latin in Europe.

*Initial from the **Grammaire de Priscien***
NINTH CENTURY, STIFTSBIBLIOTHEK, ST GALL

# Pliny the Elder

**P**liny the Elder (Gaius Plinius Secundus) was born in Como, northern Italy, where the family had estates, in AD 23. He trained as a lawyer and orator in Rome and went to North Africa when he was about twenty-two years of age. He served in the Roman army in Germany. The emperor Vespasian sent him to Spain in charge of the revenue and later the emperor Titus made him prefect of the fleet at Misenum. He visited Pompeii in AD 79 during one of the volcanic eruptions of Mount Vesuvius and was asphyxiated by clouds of gas.

Of his seven books, all but the last have been lost. This was his *Historia Naturalis* (*Natural History*), which appeared in AD 77. From the number of early manuscript copies, it seems to have been his most popular work. The earliest known copy is the Nonantulanus palimpsest, which dates from the fifth or sixth century. Since the first printing in Venice in 1469, hundreds of editions in Latin have been produced.

Our text comes from a fragment written in the first half of the eighth century in insular minuscule script and is made up of parts of Books II to VI. It was written in Northumberland, probably at one of the twin monasteries of Monkwearmouth and Jarrow, because the initials are very similar to those in the Durham Cassiodorus. Since Pliny included in his work everything pertaining to the world and to man, it was, therefore, a reference book, an *Encyclopaedia Romana*.

The illuminations on this page are versal letters from one of the lists of chapters and the openings of the Books. The initials show great verve and fantasy and are drawn in black with spirals, animal's hindquarters and human hands as terminals. The letter *T* has a hollow, curved stem, the slender base of which terminates in the rear quarters of a bird which has an animal's tail with a lobed end. The arm of the letter terminates on the left with a double-coil spiral and pelta and on the right with a human hand in the two-fingered attitude of peace.

*Initials from Voss Lat.F4*
EIGHTH CENTURY, UNIVERSITEITSBIBLIOTEK, LEIDEN

The capital *B* has the hollow stem of the lower bowl terminating in similar hind-quarters, but the crossbar is a biting bird's head whose crest continues as the hollow upper bowl of the letter to terminate in a single spiral in which are arranged five dots, like the number five on a modern dice. The hollow stem of the letter terminates at both ends in a concave serif. The letter *h* has no zoomorphic or anthropomorphic connections, as its decoration is limited to single-coil spirals.

Plinys' *Historia Naturalis* was divided into thirty-six books, some of which are listed below to show how comprehensive his work was:

Book 1 — this contained the dedicatory epistle or preface of the whole work, which was addressed to the emperor Titus Vespasian;

Book 2 — this was a treatise on the world, the elements and the stars;

Book 5 — this contained a description of Africa;

Book 7 — this concerned man and his inventions;

Book 10 — this concerned flying fowl and birds;

Book 12 — this concerned drugs and odiferous plants;

Book 15 — this concerned 'all fruitful trees';

Book 18 — this contained a treatise on the nature of corn and all sorts, together with the profession of husband men and agriculture.

Pliny also wrote of the Druids:

> *of Misselto and the priests called Druidae ... and foreasmuch as we are entered into a discourse as touching misseltoe, I cannot overpass on a strange thing thereof used in France: THE DRUIDAE (for that is what they call their Divinors, Wisemen and state of their Clergy) esteem nothing more sacred in the world than misseltoe, and the tree whereon it breeds, so it be on oak. Now this you must take by the way, these priests or clergy men choose of purpose such groves for their divine service, as stood only upon oaks; nay they solemnise no sacrifice, nor perform any sacred ceremonies without branches and leaves thereof, so as they may well enough to be named thereupon Dryidae in Greek, which signifies as much as the oak priests. Certes, to say a truth, whatsoever they find growing upon that tree over and beside the own fruit, be it misseltoe or any thing else, they esteem it as a gift from heaven and a sure sign by which that very god whom they serve giveth them to understand, that he hath chosen that peculiar tree.*
>
> *after Philemon Holland's translation, from 1600.*

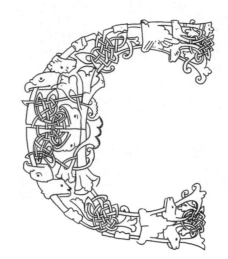

*Initial from **Bod.Auct.F.1.15***
TENTH CENTURY, BODLEIAN LIBRARY, OXFORD

# BOETHIUS

Anicius Manlius Severinus Boethius is thought to have lived from 480 AD to 524 AD. He was a Roman philosopher, orator, poet and statesman. He was sole Consul in 510 AD and was raised to the dignity of Magister Officiorum (head of the whole civil administration) by Theodoric. However, by 524 AD he had been stripped of all his honours accused of treason, and executed by Theodoric. While in prison he wrote his most influential work, *The Consolation of Philosophy*.

The copy of the work that we are interested in is that written at St Augustine's, Canterbury, in the late tenth century, and listed as Manuscript Auctarian 1.15 (S.C. 2455) in the Bodleian Library collection, Oxford. Each of the five books of the treatise is introduced by a large ornamental initial letter and is accompanied by the first words of the text in coloured capitals: silver, green, pale purple, and orange-red. The initial we have selected is the *C* on folio 5, which introduces the first book. It is drawn in brown ink with touches of red. The brown iron-gall ink was made from crushed oak apples and sulphate of iron mix, in a medium of gumarabic and water. The red colour probably came from either red lead, kermes or whelks. The initial is composed of double-line interlace, snapping animal heads and acanthus ornament, a favourite style of ornamentation of the scribes and illuminators in late tenth-century Canterbury – at least three other manuscripts have similar combinations of such features. The double-line interlace, with its 'elbow' thickenings and delicate plaited basket-work, provides an intricate background for the large biting bird and animal heads. The acanthus ornament (acanthus is a shrub from the Mediterranean region with large spiny leaves, popular with Carolingian illuminators on the continent and adopted by southern English copyists during the ninth century) is used here in a three-

*Adapted design of an initial from the opening page of* **Collestio Canonum**
EIGHTH CENTURY, DOMBIBLIOTHEK, COLOGNE

dimensional form with bulbous rings and has stylized fleshy fronds. A mid-point horizontal axis divides the *C* into two mirror images.

Boethius wrote:

> *This is the way of Pleasure*
> *She stings them that despoil her*
> *And, like the winged toiler*
> *Who's lost her honeyed treasure,*
> *She flies, but leaves her smart*
> *Deep–rankling in the heart*

*Song* **VII** *on Pleasures Sting*

# GLOSSARY

*Initial from*
***Bede's Historia***
***Ecclesiastica Gentis***
***Anglorum***
EIGHTH CENTURY,
BRITISH LIBRARY,
LONDON

| | |
|---|---|
| *anthropomorphic* | wholly or partly human in form |
| *argumenta* | prefaces in a Gospel book characterizing the Evangelists |
| *ascender* | the rising stroke of a lower-case letter |
| *capitula* | the summary of the content of a Gospel |
| *codex* | a bound book (from Latin *caudex*, tree bark); pl. codices |
| *colophon* | an inscription relating to the time, date, author, etc. of a codex; they are usually at the end of the book |
| *cumtach* | a casket or portable shrine |
| *cursive* | a handwriting form that is rapid and informal; a running hand |
| *descender* | the tail of a lower-case letter that drops below the baseline |

*Initial from Auct.DII.19*
AD 822 BODLEIAN LIBRARY,
OXFORD

| | |
|---|---|
| *diaper* | repetitive geometric pattern |
| *folio* | sheet of writing material, one half of a bifolium |
| *gloss* | a word or words commenting on the main text |
| *insular* | belonging to the culture of medieval Britain and Ireland |
| *pandect* | a complete Gospel book |
| *pelta* | abstract Celtic motif resembling a triangle |
| *serif* | an abbreviated pen stroke or device used to finish the main stroke |
| *triquetra* | a simple knot with three points formed from three intersecting arcs |
| *uncial* | a book-hand used originally by the Romans |
| *vellum* | usually refers to calf-skin |
| *versal* | a large decorative letter used to mark the opening of a line |
| *zoomorphic* | wholly or partly animal in form |

# FURTHER READING

## Books by Courtney Davis

*The Art of Celtia,* Blandford, 1994

*Celtic Art of Courtney Davis,* Spirit of Celtia, 1985

*The Celtic Art Source Book,* Blandford, 1985

*Celtic Borders and Decoration,* Blandford, 1992

*Celtic Design and Motifs,* Dover, 1991

*Celtic Image,* Blandford, 1996

*The Celtic Mandala Book,* Blandford, 1993

*Celtic Ornament,* Blandford, 1996

*The Celtic Saint Book,* Blandford, 1995

*The Celtic Tarot,* Aquarian, 1990

*The Return of King Arthur,* Blandford, 1995

## Books by Other Authors

BAINE, George,
*Celtic Art: The Methods of Construction,* Constable, 1951

BLACKHOUSE, Janet,
*The Lindisfarne Gospels,* Phaidon Press, 1981

BROWN, Peter,
*The Book of Kells,* Thames & Hudson, 1980

CARMICHAEL, Alexander,
*Carmina Gadelica,* Scottish Academic Press, n.d.

HENDERSON, George,
*From Durrow to Kells,* Thames & Hudson, 1987

HENRY, Françoise,
– *Irish Art,* Methuen, 1967
– *Irish Art in the Romanesque Period,* Methuen, 1970

LAING, Lloyd and Jennifer,
*Art of the Celts,* Thames & Hudson, 1992

MEEHAN, Bernard,
*The Book of Kells,* Thames & Hudson, 1994

NORDENFALK, Carl,
*Celtic and Anglo-Saxon Painting,*
Chatto and Windus, 1977

QUILLER, Peter, and DAVIS, Courtney,
– *Merlin Awakes,* Firebird Books, 1990
– *Merlin the Immortal,* Spirit of Celtia, 1987

ROBERTS, Forrester, and DAVIS, Courtney,
*Symbols of the Grail Quest,* Spirit of Celtia, 1990

ROMILLY Allen, J.,
*Celtic Art in Pagan and Christian Times,*
Methuen, 1993

Further details on the work of Courtney Davis can be found on his Internet web page: *http://www.wdi.co.uk/celtic/*

*Above:*
*Initial from* **The Lindisfarne Gospels**
AD 700, BRITISH LIBRARY, LONDON

# INDEX

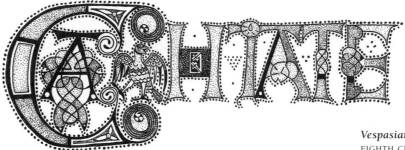

*Vespasian Psalter*
EIGHTH CENTURY, BRITISH LIBRARY, LONDON

*The following is a list of all the illustrations featured in the book and these have been arranged alphabetically according to source.*

Initials from *The Life of St Edmund, MS 776* EIGHTH CENTURY, PIERPOINT MORGAN LIBRARY, NEW YORK